Martin Hoffman has acquired a legendary reputation for his lightning-quick analysis and play of the cards. He plays professionally around the world and has a fine eye for unusual hands, those that require an unexpected move in the play.

David Bird, creator of the famous Abbot series, is the world's best-known writer of humorous bridge fiction. In 'Bridge for Money' he combines with Hoffman to relate the adventures of an American bridge pro, Jerry Blum. Sometimes the professional has to grit his teeth as a client butchers hand after hand. On other occasions Blum is playing with an expert partner against the top players in the game. Hoffman has supplied over one hundred brilliant deals and followers of David Bird will know what to expect from the narrative: a roller-coaster ride – exhilarating, hilarious and instructive.

Other books published by Finesse Bridge Publications

Bridge with Imagination – David Bird and Geir Helgemo

Norway's Geir Helgemo is rated by many as the world's top player. Runner-up in the world championship when just 23 (and again in 2001), he has won countless championships and is famed world-wide for his brilliantly imaginative cardplay. In this intriguing book he joins forces with Britain's top bridge writer, David Bird, to pass on the secrets of his success.

Having Nun, Partner? – David Bird

Enjoy the hilarious adventures of the bridge-playing nuns of St Hilda's Convent. The novices live in fear of the 80-year-old Mother of Discipline, dreading the appearance of her punishment book. Meanwhile, the first team (the Mother Superior, Sister Thomas, the Mother of Discipline and Sister Grace) face a range of colourful opponents.

Bridge Cardplay, Attack and Defence – Marc Smith

Are you tired of finishing second or third? If you could make even one extra contract per session, or beat the opponents' games just a little more often, those few additional matchpoints or IMPs would elevate you into a regular winner. Give your cardplay that extra bite by adopting the techniques described in Marc Smith's latest work.

Over Hoffman's Shoulder – Martin Hoffman and Marc Smith

Fabled cardplayer Martin Hoffman has achieved many successes in tournaments around the world, often playing as a professional with a client across the table. How does he do it? In this exciting book he joins with Marc Smith to tell the reader exactly what went through his mind as he tackled fifty great deals – from the initial bidding, right through to their triumphant conclusion.

The Magic of Bridge – David Bird and Tim Bourke

Tim Bourke is well known for his ability to create deals with a Wow! factor. In this book he and David Bird examine thirteen important areas of cardplay, passing on the requisite skills to the reader. Each technique is illustrated with both constructed deals and hands from championship play.

Bridge for Money

Tales of an American Bridge Pro

David Bird & Martin Hoffman

Finesse Bridge Publications
First published in the UK by Finesse Bridge Books Ltd 2002

ISBN 0 953 873757

Typeset by Ruth Edmondson
Cover design by Ian Wileman, cartoon by Peter McClure
Printed in the UK by Bookcraft (Ltd), Midsomer Norton

Distribution:

Worldwide (except USA): Central Books, 99 Wallis Road, London, E9 5LN. Tel +44 (0)20 8986 4854. Fax +44 (0)20 8533 5821. Email orders@Centralbooks.com

USA: Baron Barclay Bridge Supplies, 3600 Chamberlain Lane #230, Louisville, KY40241, USA. Web site http://www.baronbarclay.com Tel 1-800-274-2221 (Toll free) or (502) 426-0410. Fax (502) 426-2044.

Contents

6

1
Mrs Liebermann's Cue Bids

Jerry Blum cast an eye over the drably decorated hotel room. Is that all you got for eighty bucks nowadays? Why in Heaven's name couldn't Marty let him stay in his place as usual? So what if he had found himself a live-in girlfriend after ten years of searching. Did that mean he should bolt his doors to an old friend? These weeks away in New York were a borderline venture financially, anyway. Add half a grand to his expenses and it was barely worth the trouble.

Blum put on a blue light-weight suit, a white cotton shirt and an Italian silk tie. He always dressed smartly for his female clients. Did they want to pay two-fifty a session and have some down-and-out sitting opposite them?

Blum admired his reflection in the mirror. He could do with losing twenty pounds or so, sure, but he carried it well. He didn't have a huge beer gut bulging out over his trouser belt. No, the extra weight was evenly distributed. At a distance, if you screwed up your eyes a bit, you might even mistake it for muscle.

Blum took the hotel elevator to the ground floor and stepped out into the mid-summer blast of heat. 'Taxi!' he called. 'Cavendish at the Town Club, please. East 86th Street.'

Edith Liebermann was waiting for him in the club bar. 'Ah, Jerry, I must speak to your before we start,' she said. 'You know this five-card Stayman? Everyone is playing it here.'

Blum beckoned to the barman to bring him an iced tonic water. 'I'll play it if you like, Edith,' he replied. 'I don't recommend it particularly.'

'It is like the normal Two Clubs,' Mrs Liebermann continued. 'The response is Two Spades with five spades, Two Hearts with five hearts. I'm sure I can remember it.'

'What continuations do you want over Two Diamonds?' Blum asked. 'To find the 4-4 fits.'

Edith Liebermann reached uncertainly for her glass of fresh orange juice. Find the 4-4 fits? Five-card Stayman is to look for 5-3 fits, surely? 'I didn't hear that much,' she replied. 'I was listening to Mitzi discussing it with Ronnie Wise. Such a busy pro that Ronnie is – two sessions every day, he plays. I'm surprised he can fit a poor player like Mitzi into his schedule.'

'Take your seats, please,' called a voice from the cardroom.

Blum rose to his feet, delivering one of his well-practised client's smiles. 'Let's play the usual four-card Stayman,' he said. 'We've always done well with it in the past.'

The afternoon duplicate, played on the fourth floor, was soon under way. This was an early deal:

```
North-South Game         ♠ 7
Dealer North             ♡ A 8 3 2
                         ◇ A J 7 6 4
                         ♣ A K 2
         ♠ Q                              ♠ K 10 3 2
         ♡ 10 9 6          N              ♡ K Q J 5
         ◇ K 10 9 3      W   E            ◇ 8 5 2
         ♣ Q 10 8 5 4      S              ♣ 7 6
                         ♠ A J 9 8 6 5 4
                         ♡ 7 4
                         ◇ Q
                         ♣ J 9 3
```

West	North	East	South
Roseanne	**Edith**	**Walter**	**Jerry**
Langer	**Liebermann**	**Langer**	**Blum**
-	1◇	Pass	1♠
Pass	2♡	Pass	4♠
Pass	5♠	All Pass	

West led ♡10 and Mrs Liebermann spread out the dummy. 'With my normal partners I would have passed Four Spades,' she explained to the opponents. 'Jerry is such a card-player, you will see. I had to make one slam try.'

'Thank you, Edith,' said Blum. One trump for him and a minimum reverse? Jeez! Even the more sensible contract of Four Spades would have needed some work. 'Play the ace, will you?'

A low trump from dummy brought an unhelpful two from East. Blum rose with the ace, dropping the queen from West. He then led the queen of diamonds, pleased to see West cover with the king. He won with dummy's ace of diamonds and threw his heart loser on the diamond jack. A diamond ruff returned the lead to the South hand and Blum then played the nine of trumps to East's ten.

A club switch would have been awkward at this stage but Blum was not in the least surprised to see the king of hearts appear on the table. He ruffed in his hand and surveyed this end position:

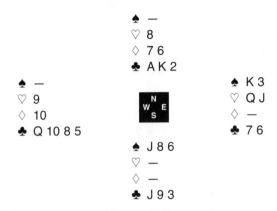

Blum continued with the jack of trumps. 'Heart away, please, Edith,' he said.

Walter Langer, the elderly East player, won with the king and forced declarer yet again in hearts. It brought him no joy. When Blum drew East's last trump with the eight, West was squeezed in the minors. It had been a bumpy journey but eleven tricks were before him.

'Only eight points, you had,' Edith observed. 'Another king and a slam would have been easy.'

Blum thought back to the six-card end position. Was he imagining it or could East have defeated him by allowing the jack of trumps to win? If he crossed to the club ace to ruff a diamond good, East could kill the entry to dummy by ditching his last club. Yes, and if he played a second round of trumps instead, he would have to throw a diamond from dummy. East could then beat him with a club return. There would be no convenient entry to the South hand to play the squeeze card. Amazing!

Walter Langer scratched the back of his balding head. 'I did everything I could,' he said. 'A heart at every stage to force his trumps. Without that defence, it would be easy.'

Blum nodded politely. There was no percentage in pointing out that an early club switch would have sunk him. No, just let the afternoon slide by and pocket the cheque.

On the next round another elderly married couple arrived at the table, Sol and Miriam Hazen. Blum was soon in game once more.

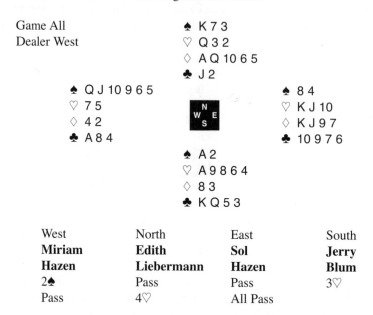

Game All
Dealer West

♠ K 7 3
♡ Q 3 2
◇ A Q 10 6 5
♣ J 2

♠ Q J 10 9 6 5
♡ 7 5
◇ 4 2
♣ A 8 4

♠ 8 4
♡ K J 10
◇ K J 9 7
♣ 10 9 7 6

♠ A 2
♡ A 9 8 6 4
◇ 8 3
♣ K Q 5 3

West	North	East	South
Miriam	**Edith**	**Sol**	**Jerry**
Hazen	**Liebermann**	**Hazen**	**Blum**
2♠	Pass	Pass	3♡
Pass	4♡	All Pass	

Blum had noticed a momentary hesitation from his partner over the weak two opening. Still, he could surely justify a bid with a six-loser hand and five cards in the other major. Passing out the weak two was certain to be a bad board.

Edith raised him to game and the queen of spades was led. Blum won with the ace and played a club to the jack, followed by a second club to the king. West won with the ace and persisted with the jack of spades, taken in the dummy. Blum paused to assess his prospects. West had shown up with seven points in the black suits already, so the red kings were surely both with her partner. West had missed the diamond switch fortunately, so there was a good chance of an endplay on East.

Blum ruffed dummy's last spade, East throwing a diamond, and drew a round of trumps with the ace. The queen of clubs stood up, leaving these cards still to be played:

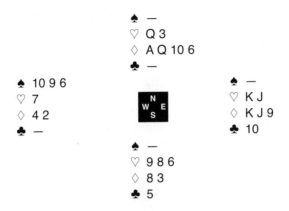

♠ —
♡ Q 3
◇ A Q 10 6
♣ —

♠ 10 9 6
♡ 7
◇ 4 2
♣ —

♠ —
♡ K J
◇ K J 9
♣ 10

♠ —
♡ 9 8 6
◇ 8 3
♣ 5

When Blum advanced his last club West ruffed with the seven. He overruffed with dummy's queen and called for a low trump. East was able to score two trump tricks but he then had to lead into dummy's diamond tenace. The game had been made.

There was nothing Sol Hazen hated more than being endplayed. 'Come a diamond through, Miriam,' he exclaimed. 'A diamond through and he has no chance.'

His wife's mouth fell open. 'You gave me a high-low in spades, Sol,' she replied. 'The spade eight, you gave me. That says play another spade.'

'Is it better I play the low card, to look like a singleton?' Sol Hazen persisted. 'Just look at the dummy. The ace-queen there will tell you what to do.' He turned towards Blum. 'You are down on a diamond switch?'

'I'd need to pick up the trumps for one loser,' Blum replied. 'The intra-finesse is best, I think. I'd run the nine first and then lead the queen, hoping to pin a doubleton jack or ten in the West hand.'

'King-jack-ten I have,' said Sol Hazen. 'Your intra-finesse can pick this up?'

Blum shook his head and Hazen delivered another pained look across the table. 'Come a diamond like I said, Miriam. He must go down.'

The next few rounds went well and Blum had every confidence in delivering a good score for his client. Round 7 saw the arrival of two women who were well known to Blum. Both widowed for several years, they played so much duplicate together they were practically residents at the club.

'Ah, Jerry,' said the effervescent Linda Glover, taking her seat. 'Nice to see you again. Why so long? You don't like New York any more?'

'Of course I do,' Blum replied. 'Where else can you find such attractive women?'

The three ladies laughed. 'Such a flatterer, he is,' Linda declared. 'Why, Edith, I bet he even tells you that you're a good bridge player.'

The smile froze on Edith's face. 'If Jerry says that, it's because he means it. We do very well together.'

Blum was the dealer on the first board of the round:

Love All
Dealer South

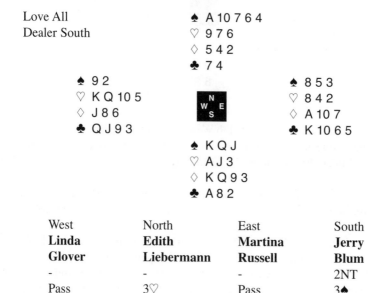

```
                    ♠ A 10 7 6 4
                    ♡ 9 7 6
                    ◇ 5 4 2
                    ♣ 7 4
 ♠ 9 2                              ♠ 8 5 3
 ♡ K Q 10 5              N          ♡ 8 4 2
 ◇ J 8 6             W       E      ◇ A 10 7
 ♣ Q J 9 3               S          ♣ K 10 6 5
                    ♠ K Q J
                    ♡ A J 3
                    ◇ K Q 9 3
                    ♣ A 8 2
```

West	North	East	South
Linda	**Edith**	**Martina**	**Jerry**
Glover	**Liebermann**	**Russell**	**Blum**
-	-	-	2NT
Pass	3♡	Pass	3♠
Pass	3NT	Pass	4♠
All Pass			

A transfer auction carried Blum to Four Spades and Linda Glover led the king of hearts. Blum surveyed the dummy thoughtfully. It seemed he had done the right thing by not playing in 3NT. Mind you, the spade game was not exactly cold either. To have any chance he would have to set up a discard on the diamond suit.

Blum allowed the heart king to win the first trick. Linda Glover, who had noted her partner's discouraging two, switched to the queen of clubs. Blum, who had no wish for East to gain the lead and play a heart, allowed this card to win also. He won the club continuation and drew trumps, overtaking the jack with the ace on the third round. A diamond to the king held the next trick and he re-entered dummy with a club ruff to lead another diamond. East ducked again and the queen won.

When Blum played another diamond the suit broke 3-3. 'I have ten tricks now' he said, facing his remaining cards. 'Five trumps, three diamonds and two aces.'

Edith nodded approvingly as she inspected the scoresheet. 'You see how well we do together, Linda?' she said. 'Most pairs have gone down.'

'One down? It's not possible,' declared Linda. 'There's a discard on the long diamond. We had no chance to beat it.'

Edith looked hopefully across the table. 'Could they have defeated it?' she asked.

'Well, it wasn't easy,' replied Blum hesitantly, 'but maybe...'

'Don't be shy, tell us,' said Martina Russell. 'How can we beat it?'

'Suppose Linda switches to a trump instead of the club queen,' Blum continued. 'I have only one entry to dummy to lead towards the diamonds. If I duck a club, to set up a second ruffing entry, Martina can win and play a heart through.'

'Yes, a trump switch,' Martina exclaimed. 'Do you see, Linda? I was hoping you would find that.'

Linda Glover was not greatly pleased by Blum's analysis. 'Is that the only chance of beating it?' she said.

'Well, again it's difficult,' continued Blum, 'but if Martina overtakes your queen of clubs with the king I'm in trouble. If I duck, she can play a heart; if I don't, I have only one entry to play towards the diamonds.'

Linda looked triumphantly across the table. 'Yes, overtake with the king,' she said. 'I was hoping you would find that defence, Martina.'

The last round of the session saw the arrival of fellow professional, Ronnie Wise at Blum's table. He gave Blum a wink as he took his seat. 'Aren't we the lucky ones?' he said. 'We get a date with an attractive lady. Our wives don't mind and we get paid for it!'

Mitzi Albrecher, who was wearing enough jewellery to stock a small shop, lowered herself into the East seat. 'Such a good session we have had,' she declared. 'Don't you spoil it for us, Jerry.'

'And don't you spoil our good session,' said Edith. 'Only one bad board we have had and there was nothing we could do about it. Not with the opening lead I got, anyway.'

Wise scored well in 1NT on the first board and Blum was looking to end the session with a good result as he picked up these cards:

♠ A K 7 6 4 3
♡ K Q 4
◇ —
♣ K Q 10 2

Edith opened 1◇ and rebid 1NT over his 1♠ response. This was a weak rebid, showing 12-14 points. Blum bid a forcing 3♠ and perked up when he heard a cue bid of 4♣ opposite. There would be a small slam at least, now. He cue-bid 4◇ and was pleased to hear 4♡. Surely there would be no losers outside the trump suit, he thought. What was the worst trump holding on which Edith would cue-bid? Three to the queen? Even if she had three to the jack or queen doubleton, there would be fair play for a grand. Yes, let's end with a bang. Seven Spades, it must be!

The diamond ace was led and this proved to be the full deal:

North-South Game
Dealer West

```
                    ♠ 10 2
                    ♡ A 10 8 3
                    ◇ Q J 9 6 4
                    ♣ A J
    ♠ 9 8 5                        ♠ Q J
    ♡ 9 5 2          N             ♡ J 7 6
    ◇ A K 5 3      W   E           ◇ 10 8 7 2
    ♣ 8 6 3          S             ♣ 9 7 5 4
                    ♠ A K 7 6 4 3
                    ♡ K Q 4
                    ◇ —
                    ♣ K Q 10 2
```

West	North	East	South
Mitzi	**Edith**	**Ronnie**	**Jerry**
Albrecher	**Liebermann**	**Wise**	**Blum**
Pass	1◇	Pass	1♠
Pass	1NT	Pass	3♠
Pass	4♣	Pass	4◇
Pass	4♡	Pass	7♠
All Pass			

'Such a nice chance for using the cue bids,' Edith declared, as she laid out the dummy. 'My normal partners don't play them.'

Blum could not believe the dummy's trump holding. With only ten-one of trumps, she cue-bids? The contract was absolutely hopeless. No chance whatsoever, unless... what if he could ruff four diamonds in his hand, score six winners in hearts and clubs, and ruff a club with the ten at Trick 11. If the cards lay just right, the trump queen-jack lying with the last club, perhaps it could be done.

Blum ruffed ◇A and crossed to ♣J to ruff another diamond. A club to the ace permitted a third diamond ruff. Three rounds of hearts stood up, followed by a fourth diamond ruff and ♣K. These cards remained:

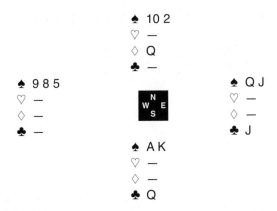

When ♣Q was led, the required miracle occurred. West was out of clubs but held no trump higher than dummy's ten. Blum overruffed West's five with the ten and faced his trump ace-king to claim the last two tricks.

'Only with cue-bidding we could get there!' exclaimed a delighted Edith Liebermann. Her smile widened as she inspected the travelling scoresheet. 'No-one else found the grand. Not one other pair.'

The two pros pocketed their cheques and shared a cab to the Honors Club in 57th St, where they both had clients lined up for the evening game.

'I still can't believe that grand!' Wise exclaimed, as the yellow cab sped along Park Avenue, weaving from lane to lane. 'Mitzi's diamond lead must be the only one to let it through.'

'No, I make it on a heart or club lead,' Blum replied. 'I can ruff a club winner for the extra entry.'

'That's true,' said Wise. 'A trump lead must beat it, of course.' .

'That's right,' agreed Blum. 'I can't use a club ruff as an entry then, because only the trump ten would be left.'

Wise gave a rueful shake of the head. 'With the diamond ace in her hand Mitzi must have thought you'd bid the grand with a top loser.'

Blum laughed. 'That's not possible,' he said. 'Not when you have a top-class pair using cue bids!'

2
Winter in the Big Apple

Half a block from the Honors Club was an excellent delicatessen. Blum and Wise took a table by the window and enjoyed a pastrami on rye, followed by a strong coffee. Resisting the temptation to repeat the order, they walked the last few yards to the club and arrived in respectable time. Blum's client was already there, enjoying a bourbon at the bar.

'Hi Rick,' said Blum. 'Still in business?'

'Hangin' on, yeah,' Rick Winter replied. 'Wanna join me?'

'Just a tonic water, thanks,' Blum replied. 'Don't like to drink when I'm working.'

Winter relayed the order to the barman, who had it ready in the blink of an eye. Winter slid the glass to Blum. 'How's Jeanette?' he asked. 'You two still speakin' to each other?'

'Actually, no,' Blum replied. 'We split a couple of months back.'

'Sorry to hear that,' said Winter. 'Lucille will be too.'

'Probably for the best,' said Blum, peering down into his glass. 'Life goes on.'

'Plenty of other fish to fry,' said Winter. 'Enjoy your freedom! That's my advice.'

Blum, who had three failed marriages behind him, managed a weak smile. Freedom wasn't worth very much at his age, not when you had to pay for the privilege by cooking your own meals and ironing your own shirts.

The players moved to the cardroom and play began. This was an early board at Blum's table:

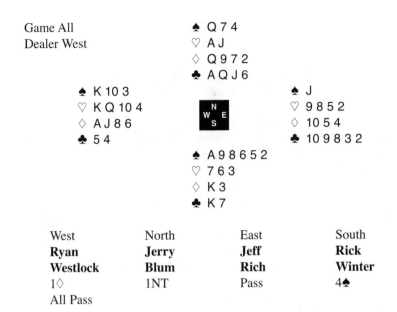

Game All
Dealer West

        ♠ Q 7 4
        ♡ A J
        ◇ Q 9 7 2
        ♣ A Q J 6

♠ K 10 3   ♠ J
♡ K Q 10 4   ♡ 9 8 5 2
◇ A J 8 6   ◇ 10 5 4
♣ 5 4   ♣ 10 9 8 3 2

        ♠ A 9 8 6 5 2
        ♡ 7 6 3
        ◇ K 3
        ♣ K 7

West	North	East	South
Ryan	**Jerry**	**Jeff**	**Rick**
Westlock	**Blum**	**Rich**	**Winter**
1◇	1NT	Pass	4♠
All Pass			

Blum raised a resigned eyebrow as his partner jumped to 4♠. Why not use a transfer response and let the pro play it? Playing with Rick, that was too much to expect. He wasn't laying out a couple of entry fees and two-fifty on the side, just to sit and be dummy all night.

The king of hearts was led and Winter paused to make a plan. There were only fourteen points out, so West surely held the king of trumps. Unless the trumps broke 4-0, he could simply play ace and another trump towards the queen. He didn't need a heart ruff because his third heart could be thrown eventually on dummy's club suit. Yes, unless trumps were 4-0 there were only three possible losers – a trump, a heart and a diamond.

'Don't look so worried, partner,' said Winter jovially. 'Everything's under control.'

'I'm not worried,' Blum replied. 'I'm expecting a top with you as declarer.'

'Win with the ace,' said Winter. 'And play a low trump.'

The jack of trumps appeared on his right and he won with the ace. He was about to lead a second round of trumps towards dummy when a nasty thought occurred to him. If that jack of trumps was a singleton, West would be able to rise with the trump king on the second round and then force dummy's queen of trumps with two more rounds of hearts. Not so good. That would promote West's ten of trumps into the setting trick.

What could be done? To stop West forcing dummy to ruff, it seemed that he would have to throw one of his hearts on dummy's club suit. Yes, he would then be able to ruff a third round of hearts in his hand.

Switching tracks, Winter abandoned the trump suit and played the king and ace of clubs. When he threw a heart on the club queen, disaster struck. West pounced with the trump ten and cashed the king of trumps, the queen of hearts and the diamond ace. The game was one down.

Winter looked ruefully across the table. 'Somehow I don't think that's the top you wanted,' he said. 'Could I have played it better?'

'It was a difficult one,' Blum replied.

'Yeah, but what could I have done?' persisted Winter.

'Instead of playing a trump to the ace, cross to the club king and lead a low trump towards dummy,' suggested Blum. 'If he goes in with the king, you still have a low trump in dummy to ruff the third round of hearts. If he doesn't, you play the ace of trumps next and turn to the club suit.'

'Yes,' said Winter. 'There's an even easier way to make it, too.'

'What's that?' asked Blum.

'Use a transfer bid and let you play it!'

The next few rounds went well and Blum then found himself facing Ronnie Wise. His client for the evening was Sherri Langer, a regular supporter of New York's plastic surgery industry. In a good light she could look some twenty years younger than she was.

This was the first board they played:

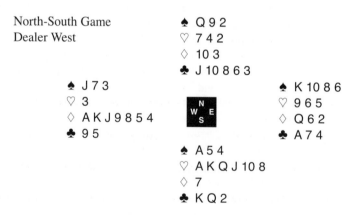

North-South Game Dealer West	♠ Q 9 2 ♡ 7 4 2 ◇ 10 3 ♣ J 10 8 6 3	
♠ J 7 3 ♡ 3 ◇ A K J 9 8 5 4 ♣ 9 5		♠ K 10 8 6 ♡ 9 6 5 ◇ Q 6 2 ♣ A 7 4
	♠ A 5 4 ♡ A K Q J 10 8 ◇ 7 ♣ K Q 2	

West	North	East	South
Rick	**Sherri**	**Jerry**	**Ronnie**
Winter	**Langer**	**Blum**	**Wise**
3♢	Pass	3NT	4♡
All Pass			

It was clear to Wise that Blum's 3NT response was a spoof. Since he had no intention of defending the obvious retreat to 4♢, he bid the heart game straight away. There was no further bidding and Winter opened the defence with two top diamonds, declarer ruffing the second round.

After drawing trumps in three rounds, Wise led the king of clubs followed by the queen. West's nine followed by the five indicated a doubleton and Blum held up the ace twice, aiming to keep declarer out of the dummy. A third round of clubs went to his ace and he exited, safely for the moment, with his last diamond. Wise ruffed and surveyed this end position:

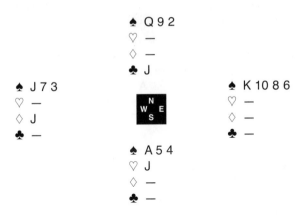

A spade to the nine left Blum endplayed. The enforced spade return was run to dummy's queen and the game was home.

'Beautifully played, Ronnie!' declared Sherri Langer. 'I had just the right cards for you.'

Wise smiled at his partner. 'I can always rely on you for that,' he replied.

'Could we have beaten it?' asked Winter.

'What happens after a trump switch at Trick 2?' said Blum. 'That leaves me with two diamonds as exit cards.'

'It's not good enough,' Wise replied. 'When I play the penultimate trump you have to keep three spades and the club ace. That means you'd have to throw one of your diamonds. I play a club to your ace and the same ending arises.'

'Yes,' agreed Blum, 'and after a spade switch at Trick 2, you cover Rick's card and duck the trick to me. Six hearts and two clubs later, I'm down to king-one of spades and the club ace, ready to be thrown in.'

'It seems that only the jack of spades lead at Trick 1 can beat it!' concluded Wise.

Sherri Langer, who had not followed a word of this analysis, looked admiringly across the table. Indeed, her features seemed to be permanently frozen in the same expression. 'Such a player Ronnie is,' she said.

This was the next board:

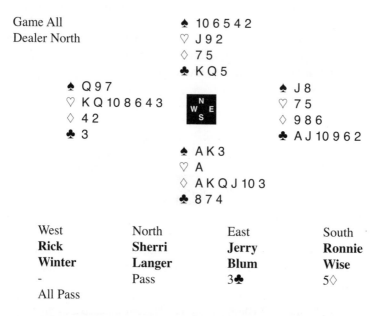

Game All
Dealer North

```
                    ♠ 10 6 5 4 2
                    ♡ J 9 2
                    ◇ 7 5
                    ♣ K Q 5
♠ Q 9 7                            ♠ J 8
♡ K Q 10 8 6 4 3                   ♡ 7 5
◇ 4 2             N                ◇ 9 8 6
♣ 3            W     E             ♣ A J 10 9 6 2
                  S
                    ♠ A K 3
                    ♡ A
                    ◇ A K Q J 10 3
                    ♣ 8 7 4
```

West	North	East	South
Rick	**Sherri**	**Jerry**	**Ronnie**
Winter	**Langer**	**Blum**	**Wise**
-	Pass	3♣	5◇
All Pass			

Blum opened 3♣ on a six-card suit, making life awkward for Ronnie Wise. With only one heart in his hand a take-out double was unattractive. Nor was 3NT played by him a very likely prospect, particularly as the lead would come through whatever dummy might hold in clubs. Reluctantly, he settled for a game in diamonds.

Winter led his singleton club and Blum captured dummy's king with the ace. When the jack of clubs was returned, Winter ruffed and exited with the king of hearts. Declarer won with the bare ace and ran six rounds of trumps. These cards remained:

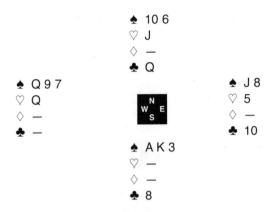

```
                    ♠ 10 6
                    ♡ J
                    ◇ —
                    ♣ Q
    ♠ Q 9 7                         ♠ J 8
    ♡ Q              N              ♡ 5
    ◇ —          W       E         ◇ —
    ♣ —              S              ♣ 10
                    ♠ A K 3
                    ♡ —
                    ◇ —
                    ♣ 8
```

A club to dummy's queen caught West in a simple squeeze. He retained the queen of hearts, guarding the threat he could actually see, and the resultant spade discard set up South's holding in the suit. The game had been made.

An amused Ronnie Wise turned to his left. 'You can beat this, you know,' he said. 'Don't ruff the club!'

'I had two baby trumps,' Winter protested. 'Of course I ruff.'

'Discard instead and you remove the queen of clubs from dummy,' persisted Wise. 'I needed that entry for the squeeze. You don't make a small trump, it's true, but you make two side-suit winners instead.'

Winter looked across at Blum. 'Is that right?' he said.

'As it happens,' replied Blum. 'Still, you couldn't tell I had only six clubs. If I had seven clubs and you didn't ruff, you'd give declarer an extra trick.'

Sherri Langer surveyed the scoresheet with no great enthusiasm. 'Four Spades and 3NT are better, Ronnie,' she said. 'When you bid Five Diamonds, there was nothing I could do.'

Wise shrugged his shoulders. 'Jerry's pre-empt made life difficult,' he replied. 'Most people around here need seven cards for a pre-empt.'

The next round saw Blum and Winter facing the oldest member of the club, Jesse Humboldt. A big man all his life, he still weighed over 240 pounds at the age of eighty-nine.

'How are you doing, Jesse?' asked Blum as he took his seat.

'Not so bad,' the old guy replied. 'I don't play as well as I used to. You know how it is, Jerry. I get tired if I put too much effort into it.'

Blum did not believe a word of this. There were few players in the club who played the dummy as well as Humboldt. His bidding was rather hit-and-miss, it was true.

On the first board of the round Blum scored well, playing in a spade part score. This was the second board:

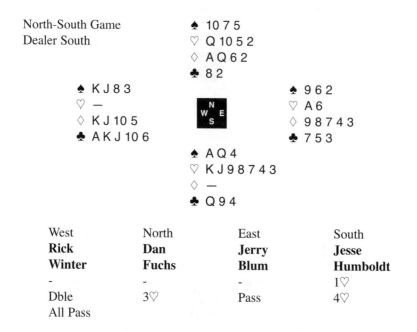

North-South Game
Dealer South

♠ 10 7 5
♡ Q 10 5 2
◇ A Q 6 2
♣ 8 2

♠ K J 8 3
♡ —
◇ K J 10 5
♣ A K J 10 6

♠ 9 6 2
♡ A 6
◇ 9 8 7 4 3
♣ 7 5 3

♠ A Q 4
♡ K J 9 8 7 4 3
◇ —
♣ Q 9 4

West	North	East	South
Rick	**Dan**	**Jerry**	**Jesse**
Winter	**Fuchs**	**Blum**	**Humboldt**
-	-	-	1♡
Dble	3♡	Pass	4♡
All Pass			

Winter led the ace of clubs against the heart game, winning the first trick. When he continued with the king of clubs, the 89-year-old declarer dropped the queen from his hand. By feigning a doubleton he hoped to induce a helpful switch from West.

Winter paused to consider his next play. Could Blum hold the spade ace? He had played a discouraging three on the first round of clubs and some middle-looking card on the second round. Holding the ace of spades, he would surely have played his highest spot-card on the second round. He still held the club nine and he could have signalled with that.

Concluding that a spade switch was too dangerous, Winter exited with the jack of diamonds. 'Play the queen.' said Humboldt.

The diamond finesse succeeded and declarer threw a spade from his hand. He then drew trumps, eventually ruffing a club and discarding the spade queen on the ace of diamonds. The game had been made.

'Difficult for you, Rick,' said Blum. 'You needed to play a third round of clubs. He has to lose a spade trick then.'

'I'm not giving him a ruff-and-discard,' Winter replied. 'If that's what was needed, I'm afraid it was just too difficult.'

'It wouldn't have been a ruff-and-discard,' said Blum. 'He had another club left.'

The enormous Jesse Humboldt leaned forward, wincing from the effort. He extracted the club queen from the line of cards before him. 'Would this be the card that fooled you?' he asked, a smile on his lips.

'That's right, the queen fell on the second round,' Winter replied. 'Did you play it on purpose?'

Humboldt shared an amused look with his partner. 'Sure did,' he said. 'Nothin' much to lose by tryin' it. The club queen wasn't any use to me, not with the spade finesse almost certain to be wrong.'

A round or two later, facing an elderly married couple, Rick Winter was once more in the declarer's seat. This was the deal:

East-West Game
Dealer South

	♠ 9 7 6 2	
	♡ 9 5 4	
	◇ K 8 3	
	♣ A 10 7	
♠ A K Q 10 5		♠ J 8 3
♡ 2		♡ 10 8 7 3
◇ Q 10 2	N W E S	◇ J 7 6 4
♣ 8 6 5 2		♣ K 4
	♠ 4	
	♡ A K Q J 6	
	◇ A 9 5	
	♣ Q J 9 3	

West	North	East	South
Freddie	**Jerry**	**Elaine**	**Rick**
Stopp	**Blum**	**Stopp**	**Winter**
-	-	-	1♡
1♠	2♡	Pass	4♡
All Pass			

'My lead?' said the white-haired Freddie Stopp, glancing at the declarer.

Winter delivered a friendly smile. 'Fire away,' he replied.

Stopp led the ace of spades and continued with the spade king. Winter ruffed and played on trumps, not overjoyed to see West show out on the second round.

If he drew all of East's trumps, exhausting his own trumps in the process, he would be unprotected in spades if the club finesse lost. Hoping to cut his losses in this situation, Winter ran the queen of clubs before drawing any more trumps. Elaine Stopp won with the king of clubs and lost no time in returning a third round of spades, forcing declarer to ruff again.

Rick Winter paused to take stock. It seemed he would still be all right if East had to follow to three more clubs and both diamonds. She would then have the dubious pleasure of ruffing her partner's diamond winner at Trick 13. That would be amusing.

Such hilarity was not to be. East ruffed the third round of clubs and the game went one down.

Elaine Stopp leaned to her right as Blum was filling out the travelling scoresheet. 'Most people made Four Hearts,' she informed her husband proudly. 'We must have defended better than the others.'

'Or I played it worse,' suggested Winter. He looked across the table. 'Anything I could have done?'

'Perhaps you could throw a diamond on the second spade,' Blum suggested. 'You're going to lose a diamond anyway, so it doesn't cost anything. You ruff the third spade, draw trump and run the queen of clubs. East doesn't have any spades left now.'

Winter looked disappointed. 'Should have seen that,' he declared. 'Despite all your efforts, Jerry, I don't think I'm ever goin' to make the Bermuda Bowl!'

'Bermuda Bowl?' queried Elaine Stopp. 'What's that?'

'We ain't going there at our age,' declared Freddie Stopp, 'Don't matter where it is.'

This was the second board of the round:

Game All	♠ Q 7 6 4	
Dealer West	♡ —	
	◇ Q 9 8 2	
	♣ K J 8 6 3	

♠ —		♠ 10 8 2
♡ K Q 9 5 4	N W E S	♡ J 8 7 6 3 2
◇ K J 7		◇ 10 6 5 3
♣ A 10 5 4 2		♣ —

♠ A K J 9 5 3	
♡ A 10	
◇ A 4	
♣ Q 9 7	

West	North	East	South
Freddie	**Jerry**	**Elaine**	**Rick**
Stopp	**Blum**	**Stopp**	**Winter**
1♡	Pass	2♡	4♠
Pass	5♡	Pass	6♠
Pass	Pass	Dble	All Pass

Placing partner with a good hand for his vulnerable 4♠ overcall, Blum made a slam try. Winter was happy to accept and Mrs Stopp doubled in the pass-out seat. Freddie Stopp had already extracted the king of hearts and saw no reason to change the lead on account of his wife's double.

'Thanks, Jerry,' said Winter, as the dummy went down. 'Throw a diamond.'

Elaine Stopp, who was glaring at her husband, followed with an exaggerated two of hearts. She was hoping to indicate what he should have led. No doubt she would tell him again later that night... and for many days to come. After drawing trumps in three rounds, Winter led the seven of clubs to the king. When East showed out, delivering another pointed look in her husband's direction, he continued with a second round of clubs to the queen and West's ace.

Freddie Stopp paused to consider his return. Did Elaine hold the diamond ace? Surely not. She had thrown two low hearts when declarer played on clubs. If she held the diamond ace she would have given a vigorous signal in diamonds. It had not escaped Stopp's attention that declarer had carelessly blocked the club suit by retaining the nine. Surely the best defence would be another round of hearts, removing an entry from the dummy.

Winter ruffed West's queen of hearts return in the dummy and crossed back to his hand with the ace of diamonds. Two more rounds of trumps brought him to this end position:

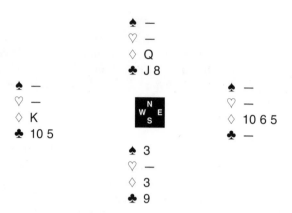

When the last spade was led, Freddie Stopp had no good discard in the West seat. Reluctantly he parted with ♣5. The diamond queen was thrown from dummy and declarer was able to overtake ♣9 with the jack to score two club tricks.

'I was squeezed, Elaine,' declared Freddie Stopp. 'Nothing I could do.'

Elaine Stopp wrote down the score in her card, marking the board with a large black cross. Nothing he could do? The right defence had been totally obvious after her Lightner double. If Freddie had led ace and another club they would he halfway through the next board by now.

Rick Winter gazed happily across at Blum. 'Did you like that one, Jerry?' he said. 'I normally leave the squeezes to you.'

There was nothing Blum liked better than a contented customer. 'Yes, it was good,' he replied. 'Another way to make it was to unblock the nine on the first round of clubs. Then you can finesse the eight.'

'You know what they say, though,' continued Winter. 'When the choice is between a finesse or a squeeze, the expert always prefers the squeeze.'

Blum laughed. 'So they do,' he said.

3
Sushi in Toronto

L ouisa Geller was waiting for Blum in the foyer of the Royal York Hotel in Toronto. Only five foot in stature, she was wearing a blue knee-length skirt and a white silk blouse. No-one would have guessed from her unimposing appearance that she was senior vice-  president of a famous frozen food company. Louisa and Blum exchanged a light embrace. They ordered some coffee and were soon busy looking over the convention card from the previous time they had played together.

In general Blum was happy to play whatever methods his clients liked. Conventions made little difference in his opinion but it was losing tactics to persuade a client to play some method unfamiliar to them.

'You remember you agreed to play that double of Three Spades my way last time?' said Louisa, peering over her gold-rimmed spectacles.

'Did I?' replied Blum 'I don't recall it at the moment.'

'One Diamond from me, they come in with One Spade, Three Diamonds from you and then Three Spades,' continued Louisa. 'I doubled, which would have been 200 and you pulled it.'

'You like that for penalties?' said Blum.

'When they are vulnerable, yes. Plus 200 would have been a top for us.'

'That's fine,' said Blum. 'So long as I know.'

A couple of hours later Blum and Louisa took their seats in the main ballroom for the first qualifying round of the Life Master Pairs. Blum looked up and down the line of players. Quite a strong section. There would be 320 qualifiers for the semi-final the following day but, contrary to Louisa's impression, it would not be a foregone conclusion to get through.

The early boards were unspectacular but on the third round a slam deal arrived. This was the board:

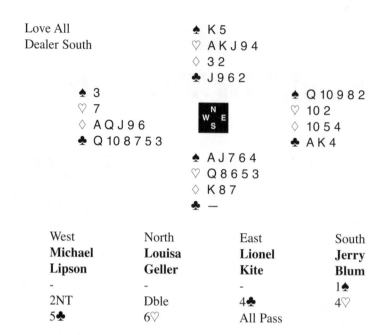

Love All
Dealer South

```
                   ♠ K 5
                   ♡ A K J 9 4
                   ◇ 3 2
                   ♣ J 9 6 2
♠ 3                                    ♠ Q 10 9 8 2
♡ 7                                    ♡ 10 2
◇ A Q J 9 6          N                 ◇ 10 5 4
♣ Q 10 8 7 5 3    W     E              ♣ A K 4
                     S
                   ♠ A J 7 6 4
                   ♡ Q 8 6 5 3
                   ◇ K 8 7
                   ♣ —
```

West	North	East	South
Michael	**Louisa**	**Lionel**	**Jerry**
Lipson	**Geller**	**Kite**	**Blum**
-	-	-	1♠
2NT	Dble	4♣	4♡
5♣	6♡	All Pass	

West led ♣7 against the small slam in hearts and Blum ruffed East's king. All followed when a trump was played to the ace. What now?

East was apparently marked with the ace and king of clubs, so West surely held the diamond ace. Blum paused to calculate what would happen if he drew the outstanding trump next. He could play the king of spades and finesse the spade jack. If spades were 4-2 he would be able to ruff the spades good. He could then throw two diamonds from dummy on the good spades and score two diamond ruffs. This line would fail if spades were 5-1, though.

Since spades would need to be 4-2 on the line he had considered, it seemed that there was nothing to be lost by playing on spades before drawing the last trump. Blum cashed the spade king and finessed the jack of spades. He knew he had done the right thing when West showed out but was unable to ruff. He played the ace of spades, throwing a diamond from dummy, and ruffed a spade. When he led dummy's remaining diamond to the king, this lost to the ace as he had expected. He could not be prevented from scoring the remaining six trumps separately, on a cross-ruff, and the slam was made.

Louisa looked proudly across the table. 'Not everyone would bid Six Hearts on my hand,' she said.

'No, it was a good bid,' replied Blum. Not everyone would make twelve tricks, of course. Not that it was his style to point this out.

'Just as well the other two pairs didn't bid six,' observed Louisa, as she entered the score. 'They didn't even manage to make twelve tricks!'

A round or two later, two serious looking men in their early thirties arrived at Blum's table. He didn't recognise them but that was no reason to expect an easy ride. In a major event like this there would be two or three hundred pairs capable of giving a good account of themselves.

'You play Standard?' asked the taller of the two, taking the East seat.

'With a few gadgets,' Louisa replied. Didn't they know who her partner was? It wasn't cheap, hiring a pro for a National, particularly with the room rate at a ludicrous 210 Canadian a night. At the very least she expected her partner to be recognised. She raised her voice. 'Jerry Blum and I like to play the latest conventions.'

The two men nodded politely and drew their cards for the first board of the round. With any luck, thought Louisa, Jerry would duff them up with a piece of expert cardplay. They wouldn't forget playing against him then!

```
East-West Game          ♠ 10 7 4
Dealer West             ♡ A J 10 6 2
                        ◇ 3 2
                        ♣ A 6 4
        ♠ K J                               ♠ 9 2
        ♡ Q 8 7 5            N              ♡ K 9 3
        ◇ K Q J 9        W       E          ◇ 10 8 7 6 4
        ♣ K J 9             S              ♣ 10 7 5
                        ♠ A Q 8 6 5 3
                        ♡ 4
                        ◇ A 5
                        ♣ Q 8 3 2
```

West	North	East	South
Dennis	**Louisa**	**Stefan**	**Jerry**
Lobert	**Geller**	**Syrkin**	**Blum**
1NT	Pass	Pass	2♠
Pass	4♠	All Pass	

West led the king of diamonds and down went the dummy. Blum surveyed the meagre nine-count. Four Spades she says, on that? It was just as well he had a bit extra himself; he would have made the same bid without the ace of diamonds. 'Thanks, Louisa,' he said. 'Play the two, please.'

Blum allowed the diamond king to hold and won the diamond continuation. When he led his singleton heart West played low without any thought. Surely the guy would have split if he held the king-queen, thought Blum. He couldn't risk playing low at pairs. And if East held one of the heart honours West must hold almost everything else. 'Play the ace,' he said.

Blum continued with the jack of hearts, which East covered with the king. He ruffed in the South hand and played the ace of trumps, pleased to see the jack appear on his left. A trump to the bare king left West with no easy exit. A club would run to declarer's queen and the queen of hearts would be ruffed, setting up dummy's heart suit. The West player looked thoughtfully at his remaining cards. What if he played a low heart to dummy's ten? That was no good. Declarer would throw one club and then endplay him with a fourth round of hearts, throwing another club.

With no great hope, West tried the effect of a third round of diamonds, giving a ruff-and-discard. Blum ruffed with dummy's last trump and threw a club from his hand. He then led the ten of hearts to West's queen, throwing another club loser. West could exit safely in diamonds but when Blum ruffed and played his remaining trumps, this position arose:

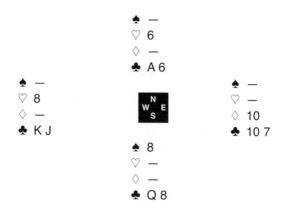

Blum's last trump squeezed West and after a long struggle the game had been made.

Louisa looked triumphantly across the table. 'How many players would find a bid of Four Spades on my hand?' she exclaimed. 'So much rubbish people talk about protective bids. When I have a raise, I raise to the full value of my hand.' She opened the travelling scoresheet, nodding happily as she surveyed its contents. 'Everyone else in a partscore!' she exclaimed 'Can you believe it?'

Blum glanced at the scores, noting that plus 170 would have been a near top anyway. Why risk a bottom by bidding game? That was the right question to ask.

The next few rounds ticked by with a succession of mundane games and part scores. Blum then picked up a good hand:

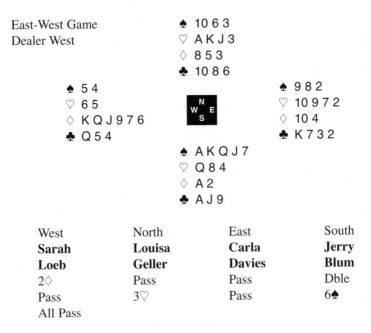

East-West Game
Dealer West

North
♠ 10 6 3
♡ A K J 3
◇ 8 5 3
♣ 10 8 6

West
♠ 5 4
♡ 6 5
◇ K Q J 9 7 6
♣ Q 5 4

East
♠ 9 8 2
♡ 10 9 7 2
◇ 10 4
♣ K 7 3 2

South
♠ A K Q J 7
♡ Q 8 4
◇ A 2
♣ A J 9

West	North	East	South
Sarah	**Louisa**	**Carla**	**Jerry**
Loeb	**Geller**	**Davies**	**Blum**
2◇	Pass	Pass	Dble
Pass	3♡	Pass	6♠
All Pass			

West opened with a weak two in diamonds and a crisp auction carried Blum to a small slam. The diamond king was led and Louisa faced her dummy. 'I'd have to bid 2♡ with four small hearts,' she observed. 'With three trump honours I had to make a jump response.'

'Nice bid,' said Blum. A simple 2♡ response was enough on her hand, particularly opposite a protective double. Still, at least there was some play for the contract. What was the best chance?

Blum drew two rounds of trumps, both defenders following. If he drew the last trump and played four rounds of hearts to discard the diamond loser, he would only be able to lead clubs once from the dummy. He would therefore need to find East with both club honours. That wasn't very good odds. The opponents were vulnerable against not and West might have chosen not to open on a bare six-count.

Blum decided to play on hearts without drawing the last trump. If the suit had broken 3-3, he would have had no option but to draw the last trump before playing a fourth round of hearts. As the cards lay, West showed out on the third heart but was unable to ruff. Blum cashed dummy's last heart and threw his losing diamond. He then played a club to the jack.

West won with the club queen and returned the queen of diamonds. Blum ruffed flamboyantly with the queen and led ♠7 to dummy's ♠10, drawing East's last trump. 'Play the club eight,' he said.

A second club finesse proved successful and the slam was home.

'If I respond with a feeble 2♡ we don't get there,' said a delighted Louisa. She opened the scoresheet, pleased once more with what she saw. 'Only two other pairs bid the slam,' she said. 'Not a very good standard here, I must say. One declarer actually went down!'

I'm surprised the other guy made it, thought Blum. It was a difficult hand to play. A kind word on his cardplay would have been welcome but... well, by the time the National was over, Louisa wouldn't have much change out of twenty grand. She was entitled to take the credit for any good results that came their way. 'You bid it well, Louisa,' he said.

The first round of the Life Master Pairs was fought over two sessions. Blum and Louisa picked up a healthy 54.1% on the first session and would be through to the semi-finals with any respectable effort in the evening.

'Shall we dine in the Beni-Haha?' suggested Louisa. 'I don't like to leave the hotel, as you know.'

'That's fine,' agreed Blum. 'I'm going to take a quick shower. I'll meet you in the lobby in twenty minutes.'

Louisa had reserved a prominent table for two in the hotel's Japanese restaurant. If she was paying for the best, why not let as many people as possible know about it? For her, the company of a top-class professional was worth more than wearing a Cartier necklace.

The light portions served by the restaurant suited Blum, who never ate heavily during a big event. He restored his concentration with a double espresso and was feeling in good shape as the second session of the qualifying round began.

There was not long to wait before the first big hand at Blum's table.

North-South Game
Dealer South

```
                  ♠ K Q 2
                  ♡ 4
                  ◇ A K 3 2
                  ♣ K Q 9 6 2
  ♠ 9 8 6 3                      ♠ A 10 7
  ♡ 9                            ♡ K J 10 8 7 5 3
  ◇ Q 8 7 5        N             ◇ 6
  ♣ J 8 7 4      W   E           ♣ 10 3
                   S
                  ♠ J 5 4
                  ♡ A Q 6 2
                  ◇ J 10 9 4
                  ♣ A 5
```

West	North	East	South
Margi	**Louisa**	**Geoff**	**Jerry**
Hanson	**Geller**	**Hanson**	**Blum**
-	-	-	1◇
Pass	2♣	3♡	Pass
Pass	4NT	Pass	5♡
Pass	6◇	All Pass	

Louisa carried the bidding to a small slam in diamonds and ♡9 was led. 'Such an obvious Key-card Blackwood bid,' said Louisa. 'If you'd shown three aces, I would ask for the trump queen and bid a grand.'

Blum delivered his well-practised client's smile. 'Nice dummy, Louisa,' he replied. 'Play the heart, please.'

East played low on the first trick and Blum won with the heart queen. He paused to consider his play in the trump suit. The safest play in isolation was to start with the ace in case East held a singleton queen. If the queen failed to appear, he could return to the South hand and run the trump jack. It didn't seem like a good idea here. If West held four trumps to the queen, which was more likely than normal after East's pre-empt, he would need every one of the jack, ten and nine to pick up the trump suit. In that case the four of trumps might be required to ruff the clubs good.

At Trick 2, Blum led the jack of trumps. West declined to cover and he ran the card, please to see it win the trick. The ten of trumps took the next trick, East discarding a diamond. When Blum played a spade, dislodging East's ace, the defenders were powerless. He won the spade return, cashed the ace and king of clubs and ruffed a club. He then drew trumps with dummy's ace-king and claimed the contract.

'A finesse against the queen of trumps,' declared Louisa. 'I could have played that one myself.'

A round or two later, playing against two serious looking men, Blum picked up:

♠ A 9 2
♡ A J 4 3
♢ A Q J 7 6
♣ A

With neither side vulnerable, the player to his right opened 3♣. Blum doubled for take-out and Louisa replied 3♠. What now?

He could bid 4♠, hoping that Louisa had a five-card suit. If she held only four spades, however, she would not welcome the appearance of three trumps in the dummy. She might well drop a trick or two in the play and they would get a poor score. It must be better to bid 4♢. If Louisa did hold five spades there was nothing to prevent her from rebidding the suit.

Louisa raised to 5♢, in fact, which was passed out. This was the complete deal:

Love All
Dealer East

```
                    ♠ 10 8 5 4
                    ♡ Q 6
                    ♢ K 10 9 5
                    ♣ 8 7 2
    ♠ K J 7 6                      ♠ Q 3
    ♡ K 9 8 2          N           ♡ 10 7 5
    ♢ 8 4 3         W     E        ♢ 2
    ♣ 9 5              S           ♣ K Q J 10 6 4 3
                    ♠ A 9 2
                    ♡ A J 4 3
                    ♢ A Q J 7 6
                    ♣ A
```

West	North	East	South
Arnie	**Louisa**	**Joe**	**Jerry**
Katz	**Geller**	**Redner**	**Blum**
-	-	3♣	Dble
Pass	3♠	Pass	4♢
Pass	5♢	All Pass	

Blum won the club lead and paused to consider his line of play. If East held the king of hearts a simple heart finesse would suffice. He would then be able to ruff his two remaining hearts in dummy. How did the cards lie? East was known to hold six points in the club suit. Since West might well have led a spade from a K-Q-J combination, it was a fair bet that East held one of the spade honours too. With the king of hearts in addition he would have too much for a non-vulnerable pre-empt. Yes, it was a near certainty that West held the king of hearts.

Blum drew two rounds of trumps with the ace and queen and then led a low heart from his hand. West had no answer to this. If he ducked, dummy's queen would win and declarer would proceed to ruff his two heart losers. West chose to rise with the king of hearts. When he returned a third round of trumps, Blum faced his cards and claimed eleven tricks. 'I can throw two of dummy's spades on the ace-jack of hearts,' he said, 'and eventually ruff a spade in dummy.'

'Lead a spade, Arnie!' complained the East player. 'We make two spades and a heart then.'

It seemed from the West player's weary expression that this was not the first time he had been criticised. 'Do you remember opening Three Clubs, Joe?' he replied. 'You want me to lead from a king in some other suit after you've shown a weak hand by pre-empting?'

'You knew we needed a good one,' his partner persisted. 'Two average boards wouldn't be enough to get us through.'

'Two screaming tops wouldn't be enough to get us through,' retorted the West player. 'If we score 45% we'll be lucky.'

The session drew to a close and Louisa strode triumphantly out of the playing area, arm-in-arm with Blum. An easy qualification! Why, if she played so well in the semi-final they would sail into the final. And once they reached the final... who knows what might happen?

4

Lionel Gorman's Grand Slam

Blum was awakened from his deep sleep by the phone. 'Your eight-thirty wake up call, Sir,' said a pleasant female voice at the other end.

'Thanks,' mumbled Blum, trying to sound as if he meant it.

'You're very welcome, Sir,' continued the pleasant voice. 'Have a nice day.'

For a moment Blum was tempted to take another couple of hours sleep. No, he had agreed to meet Louisa in the breakfast room at nine o'clock. Being seen taking breakfast with him was part of the deal as far as she was concerned. What was more, he was expected to be neatly dressed, shaved, and doused with a suitable after-shave lotion. There was more to being a bridge pro than bridge alone.

Blum staggered into the bedroom's en suite and gazed at the middle-aged, paunchy man residing in the mirror. Did he usually have such bags under his eyes? Only one day gone and more than a week still left. It wasn't such a strain playing with Louisa, was it? He must be getting old.

That afternoon the semi-final of the Lifemaster Pairs began. Blum and Louisa had qualified comfortably with a score of 55.3% She seemed to think they were odds-on to reach the final but Blum knew that this was a distant prospect. Easy opponents were few and far between, once you reached the semi-final of a National.

There were several early warnings of how difficult their task might be. In the fifth round they met two players from Boston, occasional acquaintances of Blum. Joseph Patton, who had the air of an expert but played an erratic game, ended as declarer on this board:

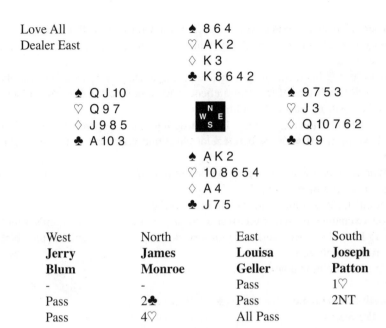

Love All
Dealer East

```
                    ♠ 8 6 4
                    ♡ A K 2
                    ◇ K 3
                    ♣ K 8 6 4 2
  ♠ Q J 10                        ♠ 9 7 5 3
  ♡ Q 9 7          N              ♡ J 3
  ◇ J 9 8 5      W   E            ◇ Q 10 7 6 2
  ♣ A 10 3         S              ♣ Q 9
                    ♠ A K 2
                    ♡ 10 8 6 5 4
                    ◇ A 4
                    ♣ J 7 5
```

West	North	East	South
Jerry	**James**	**Louisa**	**Joseph**
Blum	**Monroe**	**Geller**	**Patton**
-	-	Pass	1♡
Pass	2♣	Pass	2NT
Pass	4♡	All Pass	

Blum led the queen of spades against the heart game. Patton, whose stained fingertips bore witness to a lifelong smoking habit, thought for a while and eventually allowed the queen of spades to win. Blum continued with another spade and declarer won with the ace. A club to the king won the next trick, Louisa contributing the nine. Declarer then played two top trumps, everyone following, and cashed his remaining winners in spades and diamonds. These cards remained:

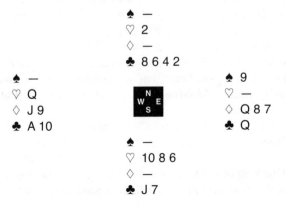

```
                    ♠ —
                    ♡ 2
                    ◇ —
                    ♣ 8 6 4 2
  ♠ —                            ♠ 9
  ♡ Q              N              ♡ —
  ◇ J 9          W   E            ◇ Q 8 7
  ♣ A 10           S              ♣ Q
                    ♠ —
                    ♡ 10 8 6
                    ◇ —
                    ♣ J 7
```

When the declarer exited with a club, Louisa had to win with the bare queen and concede a ruff-and-discard. Away went South's remaining club loser and the game was made.

Blum gritted his teeth. Why in heaven's name hadn't Louisa unblocked the club queen? It was too difficult for a client, if truth be told. Still, it was unlucky she had been sitting East and not him.

Patton turned towards Blum. 'I had a double chance there,' he said. 'You might have been left with the bare ace of clubs and your partner the remaining trump.'

'With ace-one I would go up on the first round,' Blum informed him. 'It can't be right to keep a bare honour.'

Patton smirked somewhat. 'So we just saw!' he exclaimed.

The exchange passed well over Louisa's head, much to Blum's relief. 'Nothing I could do there, Jerry,' she observed. 'A spade or a diamond, they both give a ruff-and-discard.'

This was the next board:

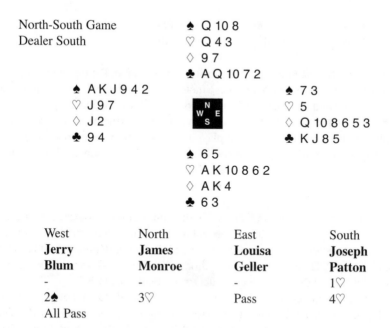

North-South Game	♠ Q 10 8	
Dealer South	♡ Q 4 3	
	◇ 9 7	
	♣ A Q 10 7 2	

♠ A K J 9 4 2		♠ 7 3
♡ J 9 7		♡ 5
◇ J 2		◇ Q 10 8 6 5 3
♣ 9 4		♣ K J 8 5

	♠ 6 5	
	♡ A K 10 8 6 2	
	◇ A K 4	
	♣ 6 3	

West	North	East	South
Jerry	**James**	**Louisa**	**Joseph**
Blum	**Monroe**	**Geller**	**Patton**
-	-	-	1♡
2♠	3♡	Pass	4♡
All Pass			

Blum led the king of spades against the heart game, drawing the seven from Louisa and the five from declarer. When he continued with the ace of spades both the closed hands followed. To kill the discard on the spade queen, Blum continued with a third round of spades. A second possible benefit of this play was that Louisa might be able to effect an uppercut, by ruffing with the ten. This would promote a trick for Blum.

A humble five of trumps appeared from East and declarer overruffed with the six. It seemed the most mundane of hands to Joseph Patton. He played the ace of trumps, preparing to claim an overtrick if the club king was onside. When East unexpectedly showed out, he paused for thought. Did that make any difference?

Patton calculated that it was no longer practicable to take a diamond ruff. Even if West followed to the first two diamonds and he managed to score the ruff, there would be no safe entry back to hand to draw the last trump. He would surely run into a trump promotion. Abandoning thoughts of a ruff, Patton drew trumps and took a deep finesse of the ten of clubs. East won with the jack and returned a low diamond to South's ace. When declarer played off his remaining trumps this end position arose:

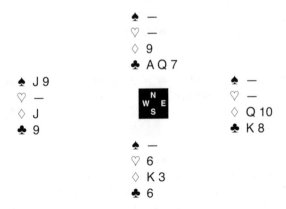

On the last trump declarer threw a club from dummy. Louisa, sitting East, had no good card to throw. Reasoning that declarer might have ruffed a diamond if he held three cards in the suit, she discarded the ten of diamonds and retained her club guard. The king of diamonds dropped the outstanding cards in the suit and the lowly diamond three became declarer's tenth trick.

Blum thrust his cards back into the wallet. Perhaps it was not going to be their day. Even when things had gone wrong for him initially, declarer had ended on his feet. There was nothing they could have done about it. If Louisa had thrown a club instead, declarer would not have been on a guess in the club suit. When he cashed the king of diamonds and continued with a club, he would know that West had two spades remaining and that the nine must therefore be his last club. It would have been obvious to drop the bare king offside.

An uninspiring mixture of good and bad boards followed. Blum estimated their score at no better than 48% when, near the end of the first session, they faced two students on this deal:

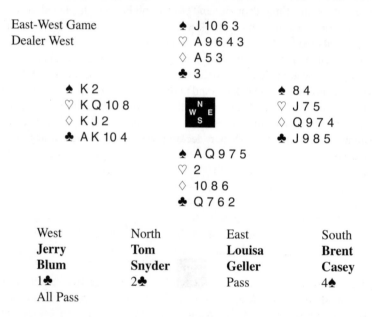

East-West Game
Dealer West

♠ J 10 6 3
♡ A 9 6 4 3
♢ A 5 3
♣ 3

♠ K 2
♡ K Q 10 8
♢ K J 2
♣ A K 10 4

♠ 8 4
♡ J 7 5
♢ Q 9 7 4
♣ J 9 8 5

♠ A Q 9 7 5
♡ 2
♢ 10 8 6
♣ Q 7 6 2

West	North	East	South
Jerry	**Tom**	**Louisa**	**Brent**
Blum	**Snyder**	**Geller**	**Casey**
1♣	2♣	Pass	4♠
All Pass			

North entered the auction with a Michaels cue bid, showing both major suits, and South leapt to Four Spades. Blum led the ace of clubs, drawing the three, five and six. He surveyed the dummy uncertainly. What should he do at Trick 2?

Blum thought back to Louisa's ♣5. With a singleton club in dummy, an expert East would give a McKenney signal on the first trick. This was not part of Louisa's methods. In any case, the club two had not yet appeared, so the five was not a clear-cut card.

Blum eventually concluded that anything but a heart was too dangerous. He switched to the king of hearts, won with the ace in dummy. 'Play another heart, will you?' said Brent Casey, who was wearing a green open-necked shirt.

The young declarer cross-ruffed three hearts and three clubs to arrive at this position, with the lead in dummy:

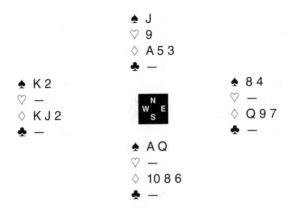

♠ J
♡ 9
◇ A 5 3
♣ —

♠ K 2
♡ —
◇ K J 2
♣ —

♠ 8 4
♡ —
◇ Q 9 7
♣ —

♠ A Q
♡ —
◇ 10 8 6
♣ —

Casey paused to consider his continuation. East had already shown up with two jacks. West's failure to switch to a diamond at Trick 2 marked her with a diamond honour as well. Since she might have found some response with around seven points, he was inclined to place the king of trumps with West. He played a trump to the ace and exited with the trump queen.

When the trumps split evenly, the game was home. Casey won the diamond switch with the ace and scored the established heart. Ten tricks were his.

'Sorry, Louisa,' said Blum. 'I needed to switch to diamonds at Trick 2. Not easy to find.'

'It needs to be a diamond honour switch,' the young declarer informed him. 'I duck a low diamond switch to the queen. If your partner returns a diamond, I cross-ruff and endplay you with the diamond king to lead into the ace-queen of trumps. If instead she plays a trump, I win with the ace and play as I just did.'

Blum was not overjoyed to receive a lecture on the game, particularly when it was accompanied by a near zero on his scorecard. 'If I switch to diamonds I play an honour, obviously,' he said.

The omens were not good when Blum and Louisa ended the first session of the semi-final with what turned out to be only a 47.8% card. 'Very disappointing,' declared Louisa. 'We played so much better yesterday.'

'The opponents played so much worse, you mean,' Blum observed. 'We played OK today. The standard is very high, that's the problem.'

After a light supper with Louisa, Blum re-fired his system with two strong cups of Colombian coffee. It was long odds against qualifying for the final after such a poor first session but he would give it his best shot.

Play restarted and Blum played the dummy well on several early boards. The sixth round saw him facing opponents who were unknown to him.

Love All

Dealer East

	♠ 4 2	
	♡ A 4	
	◊ 7 3 2	
	♣ A 9 7 6 4 3	

♠ J 6
♡ K 9 6
◊ Q 10 9 6
♣ K Q J 2

♠ 10 9 7 3
♡ Q J 5 3 2
◊ J
♣ 10 8 5

	♠ A K Q 8 5	
	♡ 10 8 7	
	◊ A K 8 5 4	
	♣ —	

West	North	East	South
Jerry	**Bruce**	**Louisa**	**Lionel**
Blum	**Trayne**	**Geller**	**Gorman**
-	-	Pass	1♠
Pass	1NT	Pass	2◊
Pass	2♠	Pass	4♠
All Pass			

A contract of Four Spades was soon reached and Blum led the king of clubs. Lionel Gorman, whose receding hair was carefully arranged to cover as much forehead as possible, won with dummy's ace. He discarded a heart from his hand and turned to his main side suit, diamonds.

When a diamond to the ace drew the jack on his right, Gorman was alerted to the fact that East might hold a singleton in the suit. He crossed to the ace of hearts and led a second round of diamonds from dummy. Louisa had no desire to ruff a losing diamond with a possible trump winner, so she discarded a club. Gorman won with the king of diamonds and surrendered a third round of the suit to West, Louisa throwing her last club. Blum cashed the king of hearts and paused to survey this end position:

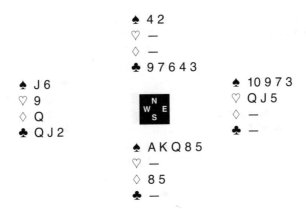

```
                    ♠ 4 2
                    ♡ —
                    ◇ —
                    ♣ 9 7 6 4 3
♠ J 6                                    ♠ 10 9 7 3
♡ 9                      N               ♡ Q J 5
◇ Q                   W     E            ◇ —
♣ Q J 2                  S               ♣ —
                    ♠ A K Q 8 5
                    ♡ —
                    ◇ 8 5
                    ♣ —
```

If Blum played his last diamond the defenders would score just one further trick, whether Louisa chose to over-ruff the dummy or not. Nor would the seemingly obvious return of a top club produce any dividend. Declarer would ruff in his hand and then ruff a diamond, setting up a long card in the suit. Again the defenders would be restricted to one trick. Strange as it seemed, Blum reckoned that the best defence would be to give a ruff-and-discard in hearts!

Gorman sat up in his seat when a heart appeared on the table. Was this good news? Suppose he took the ruff in his own hand and ruffed a diamond, overruffed by East. Whether or not the trumps had started 3-3, he would now suffer a trump promotion if East held both the remaining hearts. The alternative was to play the three top trumps, hoping for a 3-3 break in the suit.

As the cards lay, there was no way home. Gorman eventually played for an even trump break and went one down.

'Such a fright you gave me, Jerry!' Louisa exclaimed. 'With my long hearts I knew your heart play would give him a ruff-and-discard. You could not tell, of course.'

Gorman looked disdainfully at Louisa. 'Your partner defended very well,' he informed her. 'Any other defence and I make it.'

'Yes, yes,' Louisa replied. 'As the cards lie it did not cost, I realise.'

This was the next board:

North-South Game
Dealer South

♠ A K 6 2
♡ 10 7 6
◇ A Q 10
♣ A 6 5

♠ Q 5
♡ 3
◇ K J 9 7 4
♣ K J 8 4 2

♠ J 10 8 3
♡ 5 2
◇ 8 5 3 2
♣ Q 9 7

♠ 9 7 4
♡ A K Q J 9 8 4
◇ 6
♣ 10 3

West	North	East	South
Jerry	**Bruce**	**Louisa**	**Lionel**
Blum	**Trayne**	**Geller**	**Gorman**
-	-	-	1♡
2NT	Dble	3◇	4♡
Pass	4NT	Pass	5♠
Pass	7♡	All Pass	

Even though Roman Key-card Blackwood had located the three top trump honours, Blum was reluctant to lead his singleton trump. It was still possible that this might catch J-x-x-x with Louisa. He led ◇7 and down went the dummy. Blum stole a glance at the declarer, who seemed none too pleased by what he saw. 'Play the queen,' he said.

The diamond finesse succeeded and he drew trumps in two rounds. What now, thought the balding Lionel Gorman. One line was to discard a spade on the diamond ace. He could then cash the top spades and ruff a spade, setting up a thirteenth trick if spades were 3-3. This could barely be the case after West's Unusual Notrump bid, so Gorman looked for some other line. East guarded the spades. What if West held the jack of diamonds as well as the king and was alone in guarding the diamonds? Yes, there would then be a double squeeze with clubs as the pivot suit.

Gorman cashed the two top spades in dummy and continued with the diamond ace, throwing a club from his hand. He then ran the remaining trumps, soon arriving at this end position:

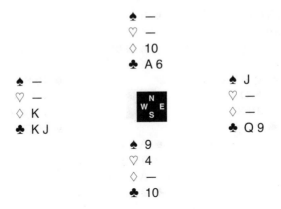

Blum had to discard the ♣J on the last trump and the diamond was thrown from dummy. Louisa had no good discard and eventually parted with a club. Dummy's ace and six of clubs scored the last two tricks and the slam had been made.

Blum winced. Since when did a performer at Gorman's level know enough to perform a double squeeze? What was worse, a club lead would have beaten it – destroying the entry in the pivot suit! Was there any reason for him to find the club lead? An expert might have responded 3♣ on Louis's cards, hoping to guide the opening lead. There was no need to bid 3♢ straight away since if they happened to be doubled in 3♣, she could retreat to diamonds later.

Louisa looked helplessly across the table. 'Nothing I could do,' she said. 'If I throw the jack of spades he makes a spade instead.'

'I know,' said Blum. 'He played it well.'

Near the end of the second session of the semi-final Blum arrived at the table of a former client of his, Maggie DeLapp. The widow of one of Boston's top art dealers, she had dispensed with Blum's services after they had failed to qualify together in some point-a-board event. Since then she had been playing with another well known pro, Bob Krasun. It didn't really matter, of course, but Blum was keen to restore his reputation by getting at least one good board on the round. The prospects of achieving this aim dipped somewhat when Krasun become declarer on the first of the two boards. This was the lay-out:

East-West Game
Dealer North

```
                    ♠ K J
                    ♡ 7 6 3
                    ◊ K Q 6
                    ♣ K Q 9 6 3
  ♠ Q 8 3 2                          ♠ 10 6
  ♡ K Q J 5          N               ♡ A 10 4
  ◊ 10 3         W       E           ◊ 7 5 4 2
  ♣ A J 5            S               ♣ 10 8 7 4
                    ♠ A 9 7 5 4
                    ♡ 9 8 2
                    ◊ A J 9 8
                    ♣ 2
```

West	North	East	South
Jerry	Maggie	Louisa	Bob
Blum	DeLapp	Geller	Krasun
-	1♣	Pass	1♠
Pass	1NT	Pass	2◊
Pass	2♠	All Pass	

Blum led the king of hearts, winning the first trick, and continued with the jack of hearts. Louisa overtook with the ace and returned a third round of the suit to Blum's queen. Blum could see two more tricks in his hand, provided the ace of clubs would stand up. What chance was there of a sixth trick for the defence?

Declarer surely held the ace of diamonds, so a trump promotion was the best idea. Blum cashed the ace of clubs and then led a fourth round of hearts, declarer throwing a club from the dummy. Blum muttered a small prayer, hoping that Louisa would see the need to ruff with her top trump. The ten of spades duly appeared from Louisa and Krasun overruffed with the ace. A finesse of the jack of trumps succeeded but East showed out on the king of trumps. Blum's remaining Q-8 in the trump suit was worth two tricks and the contract went one down.

'Excellent defence, Louisa!' Blum exclaimed. 'If you discard or ruff with the six, he makes it easily.'

'It was obvious to ruff high,' Louisa replied.

Maggie DeLapp reached sourly for the scoresheet, noting that nearly every North-South pair had made a plus score. It was typical of Jerry to play well against her. A year or two ago, when she was paying his wages, he had made hardly any effort at all.

On the next deal Bob Krasun reached a grand slam in just two bids.

Game All
Dealer North

♠ 10 2
♡ A J 10 9 7
◊ Q 3
♣ K 8 5 2

♠ 7 4 3   ♠ J 9 8 6
♡ 8 6 5 3   ♡ K Q 4
◊ 7 5 4   ◊ J 10 9 2
♣ 9 4 3   ♣ 7 6

♠ A K Q 5
♡ 2
◊ A K 8 6
♣ A Q J 10

West	North	East	South
Jerry	**Maggie**	**Louisa**	**Bob**
Blum	**DeLapp**	**Geller**	**Krasun**
-	1♡	Pass	7NT
Pass	Pass	Dble	All Pass

Blum led ♡6 against the doubled grand slam and down went the dummy.

'You open on a ten-count, vulnerable?' Krasun exclaimed.

'You said to be aggressive, Bob,' his partner replied. 'With such good hearts, of course I open.'

Krasun shook his head. 'Just this moment she chooses,' he muttered.

Blum was trying hard not to look pleased. Poor as his own hand was, it seemed that Louisa was confident of scoring a trick or two.

'Play the ace,' said Krasun. 'Small club.'

Declarer played his club winners and on the third round Louisa discarded the queen of hearts, retaining her guards in spades, hearts and diamonds. On the fourth club Louisa had to make a key discard. With no apparent clue to guide her, she released a spade.

Krasun now cashed his three top spades, brightening somewhat when the remaining cards in the suit divided 3-3. This position remained:

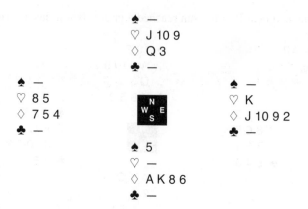

```
              ♠ —
              ♡ J 10 9
              ◇ Q 3
              ♣ —
♠ —                          ♠ —
♡ 8 5          ┌─────┐       ♡ K
◇ 7 5 4        │ N   │       ◇ J 10 9 2
♣ —            │W   E│       ♣ —
               │  S  │
               └─────┘
              ♠ 5
              ♡ —
              ◇ A K 8 6
              ♣ —
```

When Krasun led his last spade, throwing a heart from dummy, Louisa was caught in the second half of a repeating squeeze. She discarded a diamond and declarer then scored four tricks in the diamond suit, making the grand slam.

'You see!' shrieked Maggie DeLapp. 'Do I know when to open a ten-count or don't I? This must be a top for us.'

Krasun smiled broadly at her. 'It needed quite a bit of playing,' he said.

For a short moment Blum closed his eyes. It had been far too difficult a deal for Louisa to defend accurately. Had she discarded a diamond instead of a spade, though, the grand would have gone down. She would set up declarer's fourth diamond, for a twelfth trick, but dummy would have no entry remaining. The long diamond could not act as a further squeeze card and declarer would be one trick short.

Louisa left the playing area, a somewhat dispirited Blum by her side. 'We've done enough, do you think?' she asked.

'No, we're well short,' Blum replied. 'Sorry, I wanted to get through, the same as you.'

'Ah well, perhaps we'll do better in the Spingold,' said Louisa. 'We were unlucky last year, meeting that team from Texas.'

Blum never ceased to be amazed by the things clients said. Unlucky? By some miracle they had reached the last 16 last year. Didn't she realise how difficult that was? Particularly with a sponsor in a team of only four players.

A far-away look came to Louisa's eyes. 'Imagine if we reached the semi-finals or finals and had to play against Meckstroth and Rodwell. What a story I would have to tell my friends.'

Blum smiled to himself. Yes, that would be quite a story.

5
Not One American

The main teams event of the Summer Nationals in Toronto was the Spingold Knockout. There were several teams containing a playing sponsor and most of these had three pairs. Should they find themselves adrift after the sponsor had played the required number of boards, the two all-professional partnerships would play the remainder of the match, attempting to repair the damage.

Louisa liked to play all the time. She would partner Blum and their team mates would be the LA professionals, Marty Bechman and Larry Smith. A second advantage of this arrangement, from Louisa's point of view, was that she had to pay only three fees instead of five. All the teams received a seeding and the Geller team had been assigned position 26, which should mean a relatively easy draw in the first round.

The phone in Blum's hotel room sprang to life. 'Hi Jerry, it's Marty,' said the voice at the other end. 'You won't believe who we're playing today. Liekewicz's Polish team!'

'Jeez!' exclaimed Blum. 'How can they be seeded so low?'

'It's all based on US masterpoints,' Bechman replied. 'The European teams often have ridiculous seedings. Are you going to tell Louisa these Polish guys are good?'

'Better not, in case it makes her nervous,' said Blum. 'If we happen to crash out, we can put her in the picture then... just in case she thinks we lost to a bunch of idiots.'

'Yeah, that sounds best,' agreed Bechman. 'Let's hope the situation doesn't arise.'

That afternoon, the first-round Spingold matches were under way. This was an early board in the Geller-Liekewicz match:

North-South Game
Dealer North

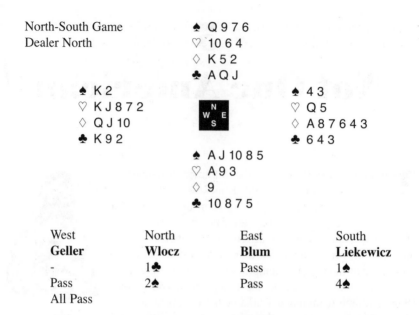

	♠ Q 9 7 6	
	♡ 10 6 4	
	◇ K 5 2	
	♣ A Q J	
♠ K 2		♠ 4 3
♡ K J 8 7 2		♡ Q 5
◇ Q J 10		◇ A 8 7 6 4 3
♣ K 9 2		♣ 6 4 3
	♠ A J 10 8 5	
	♡ A 9 3	
	◇ 9	
	♣ 10 8 7 5	

West	North	East	South
Geller	**Wlocz**	**Blum**	**Liekewicz**
-	1♣	Pass	1♠
Pass	2♠	Pass	4♠
All Pass			

Louisa led the queen of diamonds against the spade game, drawing the two, eight and nine. The sallow-skinned declarer ruffed the diamond continuation and took a successful club finesse. The spade queen was run to the king and Louisa paused to consider her next play. The defenders had no tricks to come in clubs and only one trick each from spades and diamonds. With two heart tricks needed, surely the time had come for an attack in that suit.

Liekewicz won the heart switch with the ace, drew the outstanding trumps, and repeated the club finesse. When the club king fell under the ace on the third round, he faced his remaining cards. 'One of hearts in dummy go on club ten,' he announced in a thick Eastern European accent.

It was clear to Louisa that a heart switch at Trick 2 would have beaten the game. 'I don't think you should have encouraged in diamonds, Jerry,' she declared. 'Give me a low diamond and I switch to a heart.'

'I played the eight to give you a count on the suit,' said Blum. 'There was no need to give attitude. You would know I had the ace when your queen won.'

'I don't play count signals on a queen lead,' Louisa replied. 'Discourage the diamonds and I try a heart.'

There was no point in arguing the matter and Blum entered the minus 620 in his scorecard. The Poles might, just possibly, screw up the defence at the other table but he doubted it. The game had been a thin one to bid, too. The guy sitting

South must have bid aggressively to put Louisa under some early pressure. Under that impassive exterior he was doubtless congratulating himself.

A few deals later, Liekewicz arrived in a tricky slam contract.

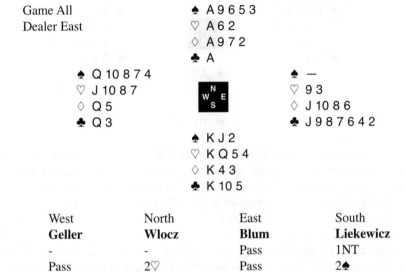

Game All   ♠ A 9 6 5 3
Dealer East   ♡ A 6 2
     ◊ A 9 7 2
     ♣ A

♠ Q 10 8 7 4   ♠ —
♡ J 10 8 7   ♡ 9 3
◊ Q 5   ◊ J 10 8 6
♣ Q 3   ♣ J 9 8 7 6 4 2

♠ K J 2
♡ K Q 5 4
◊ K 4 3
♣ K 10 5

West	North	East	South
Geller	**Wlocz**	**Blum**	**Liekewicz**
-	-	Pass	1NT
Pass	2♡	Pass	2♠
Pass	3◊	Pass	3♠
Pass	6♠	Pass	Pass
Dble	All Pass		

A transfer sequence carried the Poles to a small slam in spades and Louisa doubled on account of her good trumps. There was no further bidding and she led the jack of hearts. Liekewicz won in hand with the king, crossed to the ace of clubs and led a low trump, not particularly surprised to see East show out. After winning the trick with the trump king, he played two more rounds of hearts and ruffed his last heart. The ace and king of diamonds were followed by the king of clubs, leaving these cards still to be played:

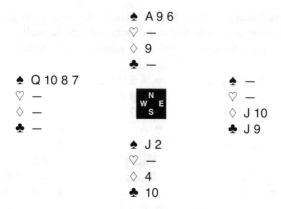

                    ♠ A 9 6
                    ♡ —
                    ◇ 9
                    ♣ —

♠ Q 10 8 7   ♠ —
♡ —   N   ♡ —
◇ —   W   E   ◇ J 10
♣ —   S   ♣ J 9

                    ♠ J 2
                    ♡ —
                    ◇ 4
                    ♣ 10

Louisa had no good answer when declarer flicked ♣10 on to the table. If she ruffed low, he would overruff with dummy's nine and exit with a diamond, forcing her to ruff and lead away from the trump queen. She eventually decided to ruff with the ten. 'Throw diamond nine,' instructed Liekewicz.

The low trump exit was run to the jack and a finesse of dummy's nine of trumps landed the doubled slam. North congratulated his partner in a flurry of incomprehensible Polish.

Louisa looked anxiously across the table. 'I had to double, didn't I?' she said. 'If I don't and they pick up 500 at the other table, it's seven IMPs away.'

Blum shrugged his shoulders. 'Most people would double,' he replied.

The first 16-board set had not gone well for the Geller team and they found themselves 29 IMPs adrift.

'We can do better than this,' Louisa informed her team-mates. 'Marty, Larry, last year you played so nicely. Come on, now. We must win the next set.'

Blum and Louisa now faced Makowski and Jagniewski, an academic looking pair who were older than their team mates. Blum had a general picture of the sort of opponents who might throw away points with careless mistakes and this was not it. Another set like the first one and the match would be nearly out of reach.

A couple of nondescript part-score boards were followed by a slam:

East-West Game
Dealer South

```
              ♠ K 7 5
              ♡ 10 4
              ◇ A K J 10 8 7
              ♣ A 9
♠ Q J 10 6 4              ♠ A 9 8 2
♡ 7 2          N          ♡ 6 5 3
◇ 4 3        W   E        ◇ Q 9 2
♣ K J 8 5      S          ♣ 10 3 2
              ♠ 3
              ♡ A K Q J 9 8
              ◇ 6 5
              ♣ Q 7 6 4
```

West	North	East	South
Geller	**Jagniewski**	**Blum**	**Makowski**
-	-	-	1♡
Pass	2◇	Pass	3♡
Pass	4♣	Pass	4NT
Pass	5♡	Pass	6♡
All Pass			

The Polish pair reached a small slam in hearts and Louisa led the queen of spades. The grey-haired Makowski paused for thought, his eyes flicking backwards and forwards between his own hand and the dummy. 'Small,' he said.

Blum paused to consider his defence. It was the same situation they had met in the first set. There was no need for an attitude signal because the position of the spade ace would be obvious by the time the first trick was completed. The right card was the nine, to give a count on his spades and let Louisa know whether another spade would stand up.

Mind you, thought Blum, it was pretty obvious that declarer held only one spade. A good player would hardly have launched into Blackwood otherwise. In fact, wait a minute... if spades were continued, declarer would ruff and draw trumps. He could then set up the diamonds with a ruff and cross to the ace of clubs to enjoy them. Yes, it was essential to remove that ace of clubs!

At Trick 1 Blum overtook the spade queen with the ace. He then switched to a low club. Makowski delivered a respectful nod in Blum's direction. The sponsor may be no great shakes but the pros surrounding her certainly knew what they were doing. He tried the queen of clubs, but this was covered by the king and ace.

Makowski threw one club on the spade king and drew trumps in three rounds. He then made the percentage play in the diamond suit, a first round finesse. Blum won with the queen and the defenders scored two club tricks for down three.

'Nice defence,' muttered the Polish declarer.

Louisa nodded. 'It's a strong point of our game,' she informed him.

Makowski soon had another taxing contract to play:

Game All   ♠ A 9 7
Dealer West   ♡ Q 9
        ◇ 8 7 6 5 2
        ♣ 7 5 2

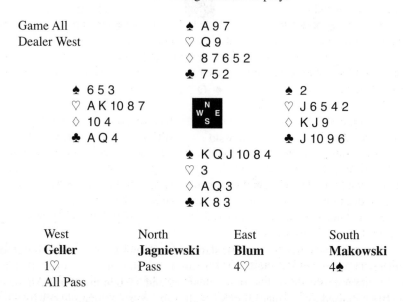

♠ 6 5 3   ♠ 2
♡ A K 10 8 7   ♡ J 6 5 4 2
◇ 10 4   ◇ K J 9
♣ A Q 4   ♣ J 10 9 6

      ♠ K Q J 10 8 4
      ♡ 3
      ◇ A Q 3
      ♣ K 8 3

West	North	East	South
Geller	**Jagniewski**	**Blum**	**Makowski**
1♡	Pass	4♡	4♠
All Pass			

Blum raised pre-emptively to 4♡ but Makowski was not hard pressed to bid 4♠ over this. There was no further bidding and Louisa led the king of hearts, drawing the nine, two and three. When she continued with the ace of hearts, the Polish declarer paused to consider the matter. West was a fair favourite to hold the diamond king but in that case the contract could be made only if she held a doubleton king and at most two trumps. After ruffing the second heart, he could play ace and a low diamond, hoping that West would win with a bare king. He could then draw two rounds of trumps, cash the diamond queen and reach dummy's good diamonds with the ace of trumps.

Makowski decided not to play for this chance. The odds of such a distribution of the cards were not especially good. Apart from that, even a sponsor might find the defence of unblocking the diamond king under the ace. East would then gain the lead on the third round of diamonds and be able to play a club through.

Trying something different, the Pole discarded a diamond on the second round of hearts. Louisa's trump switch was taken with dummy's seven and a finesse of the diamond queen succeeded. The ace of diamonds was followed by the eight of trumps to the nine and a diamond ruff with the king. A trump to the ace drew West's last card in the suit and Makowski proceeded to throw two of his clubs on the established diamond winners. He then claimed the game, losing just two hearts and a club.

'Nice line,' congratulated the Polish North. 'Ace and another diamond cannot win because West would unblock from king-one.'

Makowski gave a non-committal shrug of the shoulders, as if to say 'she would find the unblock, you think?' He reached for his scorecard and inserted a very satisfactory +620.

'Can we beat it?' asked Louisa.

'It's not easy,' said Blum. 'You need to switch to a trump at Trick 2. He's an entry short, then.'

'I was going to switch to trumps after cashing the second heart,' said Louisa.

With some difficulty Blum retained his composure. Was Louisa ever going to understand the idea of signalling count? 'I gave you the two of hearts on the first round, Louisa,' Blum replied. 'He can't have another heart.'

'Even club switch beat it!' said Makowski, smiling to himself. 'I make club king but I have still four losers.'

The Geller team had performed better in the second set but it did not stop the Polish team from gaining another 3 IMPs.

'Thirty-two down in the first round?' exclaimed Louisa, surveying her scorecard in disbelief. 'This team we are playing, they are not even American!'

Blum gritted his teeth and made no reply. You wouldn't get some weak team travelling halfway across the globe to play in the Spingold. Didn't she realise that?

The third set had not been long under way when this deal arose:

North-South Game
Dealer South

	♠ 10 7 4	
	♡ 8 5 4 2	
	◊ J 9	
	♣ 8 6 4 3	

♠ J 5 3		♠ Q 9 8 6
♡ Q J 10 9 6 3	N W E S	♡ A 7
◊ 6 3		◊ Q 8 5 4 2
♣ A 7		♣ 9 5

	♠ A K 2	
	♡ K	
	◊ A K 10 7	
	♣ K Q J 10 2	

West	North	East	South
Makowski	**Blum**	**Jagniewski**	**Geller**
-	-	-	1♣
2♡	Pass	3♡	Dble
Pass	4♣	Pass	5♣
All Pass			

The Polish pair put up a barrage but Louisa found her way into the best contract – game in clubs. The queen of hearts was led to East's ace, the king falling from declarer, and a second round of hearts was returned.

Louisa surveyed the dummy unhappily. Just one jack, Jerry had? She was paying good money for him to put down a dummy like that? Now, how could she avoid a spade loser? It seemed that the best chance was to finesse in diamonds, playing East for the queen. To get to dummy she would need to cross to the eight of trumps, so the best idea must be to ruff this second round of hearts high.

Louisa ruffed with the ten and led the trump king. Makowski played low and won South's queen on the second round of trumps. When a third round of hearts was played Louisa ruffed high again, with the jack. She then led her last trump, the two, to dummy's eight. The jack of diamonds was allowed to run and won the trick. After a second diamond to the ten Louisa claimed the contract. She had made six tricks in the side suits and five trump tricks.

'Nice play, ruffing high,' congratulated Blum. At the local club it would bring in a good score. The Poles were sure to find it, though, if they played in the same contract.

Makowski looked across at his partner, a pained expression on his face. *'Ja umieram za papierosem,'* he declared.

Jagniewski nodded sympathetically.

'*Zabronienie palania gest idiotyczne,*' continued Makowski. *'Musi sie chodzic wiecej jak kilometer zanim mozna ponownie zapalic!'*

Louisa looked quizzically at the two Poles. 'You could have beaten it, you think?' she asked.

Jagniewski laughed. 'No, he say he dying for cigarette. The most near place you are allowed to smoke is ten minutes away!'

'Unbelievable,' observed Makowski. He leaned towards Louisa. 'Spade lead would beat you,' he informed her. 'I play again a spade when I win trump ace and then partner block diamonds by covering the jack.'

Louisa smiled encouragingly at Blum. A spade lead would beat it? Larry and Marty were bound to lead a spade.

Bechman and Smith were looking happy as they returned to compare scores for the penultimate time. They had several good boards on their card and Louisa was pleased to find that the Polish lead had been cut to just 13 IMPs. 'Very good, boys!' she exclaimed. 'I am sure we can win it now.'

Blum had a chance to reduce the margin further on the very first deal of the last set:

Love All	♠ J 10 9 7 5
Dealer South	♡ 10 2
	◇ 8 4 3
	♣ 7 6 4

♠ Q 8 4	♠ —
♡ A K J 8 3	♡ Q 9 7 6 5 4
◇ K 9 5	◇ J 10 7 6
♣ Q 3	♣ K 8 5

```
         N
       W   E
         S
```

♠ A K 6 3 2
♡ —
◇ A Q 2
♣ A J 10 9 2

West	North	East	South
Wlocz	**Geller**	**Liekewicz**	**Blum**
-	-	-	1♠
2♡	2♠	4♡	4♠
Pass	Pass	5♡	5♣
Dble	All Pass		

East-West would have made their contract of Five Hearts. Blum needed little persuading to take the push into Five Spades and the Polish West's double ended the auction.

The king of hearts was led and Blum nodded his thanks as the dummy was laid out. West had no reason to expect any heart tricks in defence, so his final double suggested that he held all three trumps. To make the contract it would be necessary to set up the club suit. In order to take two club finesses, a rather spectacular play would be needed. At Trick 1 Blum ruffed the heart lead with the ace! His next move was a low trump from the South hand.

Wlocz rose with the trump queen and East showed out. Blum ruffed the heart continuation with the king and crossed to dummy's jack of trumps. A club to the jack lost to the queen and West exited passively with his last trump, won on the table. The next club finesse was successful and Blum was able to throw two diamonds from dummy on his surplus club winners. The contract of Five Spades doubled had been made.

The East player scribbled the adverse result in his scorecard. 'You see how we beat it?' he demanded of his partner.

Wlocz gave a disinterested shake of the head. Whatever his partner had in mind, it was too late.

'You must lead diamond into ace-queen!' his partner exclaimed. 'When he play on trump, you win and clear diamond trick before clubs are made good.'

Wlocz was not amused. 'Ah yes, diamond lead. I nearly found it.'

With only three boards of the final set to be played, Blum had another difficult contract to play.

North-South Game
Dealer North

	♠ 7 2	
	♡ 5	
	◊ A K 7 6 4	
	♣ A K 7 4 2	
♠ 4		♠ J 10 9 8 6 5
♡ 8 6 3	N W E S	♡ J 10 9 7 4
◊ Q J 9 5		◊ 3
♣ Q J 10 9 5		♣ 8
	♠ A K Q 3	
	♡ A K Q 2	
	◊ 10 8 2	
	♣ 6 3	

West	North	East	South
Wlocz	**Geller**	**Liekewicz**	**Blum**
-	1◇	2◇	Dble
2♡	3♣	Pass	6NT
All Pass			

Liekewicz's Michaels cue bid showed length in the majors. When Louisa made a free rebid at the three level, Blum was not to be denied a slam. He leapt to 6NT and the club queen was led, won in the dummy.

Blum paused for thought. East obviously held the sole guard in both majors but a squeeze would not yield the contract. There were only ten tricks on top, so two further tricks were required. Prospects of a 3-3 club break were almost non-existent, so it seemed that he would have to score four tricks from the diamond suit. 'Low diamond , please,' said Blum.

East played the three and Blum inserted the eight. The Polish West won deceptively with the queen and returned the ♣J. Blum won in the dummy, East discarding a spade, and paused to assess the lie of the diamonds. If East had started with ◇9 3 or a singleton ◇3, it would be safe to cross to his hand and run the ten. A worrying possibility, however, was that East had started with ◇J 3 in diamonds and West had won with the queen from ◇Q 9 5. A holding of ◇J 9 3 with East was very unlikely, since he would have made his Michaels bid on 5-4-3-1 or 4-5-3-1 shape.

Still uncertain of his intentions, Blum crossed to his hand with a spade. Marking time, he then cashed another spade. His eyes lit up when West discarded on this trick. East's shape must be 6-5-1-1. The deep finesse in diamonds was certain to succeed!

Blum led the ten of diamonds from his hand. The Polish West had read the lie of the suit and contributed an impassive five, hoping to put declarer to a guess. 'Play low,' said Blum.

East showed out, as expected, and the slam had been made.

'Just the right cards I had for you!' a delighted Louisa exclaimed.

Bechman and Smith had played another tight session at their table and the Geller team found they had won the match by 12 IMPs.

'And so I should hope,' declared Louisa, putting her scorecard into her handbag. 'What a struggle to win and they had not a single American in their team.'

Blum laughed. 'Do you know how strong they were, Louisa?' he said. 'The younger pair reached the quarter-finals of the last Rosenblum.'

Louisa was unimpressed. 'They didn't seem very good to me,' she replied. 'Particularly their bidding. Some of it... well, I couldn't understand it at all!'

6
Tilting at Windmills

Louisa's team registered fairly comfortable wins in the second and third rounds of the Spingold. They could not believe it when in the fourth round they would have to play against one of the most famous teams in bridge history – Nick Nickell's squad of Bermuda Bowl winners.

Blum's eyes were alight. 'Let's just enjoy the experience,' he said. 'Sixty-four boards against the world's greatest. There's no reason at all why we shouldn't keep the margin respectable.'

'I think we have a good chance of winning,' Louisa declared. 'A man in the bar yesterday was telling me this Nickell team is well past its best. And of course, like us, a sponsor will be playing.'

Blum listened politely. Was Louisa placing herself in the same bracket as Nick Nickell? He played a stronger game than many of the so-called professionals in other teams.

'Their sponsor is playing in the first set,' Louisa informed her team mates excitedly. 'We must take advantage of it and establish a useful lead.'

The first set saw Blum and Louisa facing Hamman and Soloway. This was an early board:

East-West Game
Dealer South

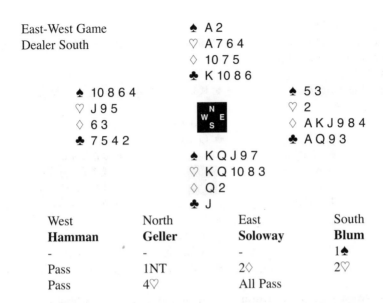

♠ A 2
♡ A 7 6 4
◇ 10 7 5
♣ K 10 8 6

♠ 10 8 6 4
♡ J 9 5
◇ 6 3
♣ 7 5 4 2

♠ 5 3
♡ 2
◇ A K J 9 8 4
♣ A Q 9 3

♠ K Q J 9 7
♡ K Q 10 8 3
◇ Q 2
♣ J

West	North	East	South
Hamman	**Geller**	**Soloway**	**Blum**
-	-	-	1♠
Pass	1NT	2◇	2♡
Pass	4♡	All Pass	

Bob Hamman led the six of diamonds and his partner scored the two top cards in the suit, everyone following. Although it was only Trick 3, the key point of the deal had been reached. If Soloway continued immediately with a third round of diamonds, declarer could avoid a trump promotion by discarding his singleton club.

Soloway spent a moment or two considering his play to the third trick. If declarer's shape was 5-5-2-1, which was quite likely, the best defence would be to cash the club ace and then play a third round of diamonds, seeking a trump promotion. Could such a defence give declarer the contract if his shape was 5-4-2-2 instead? Only if his trumps were as good as K-Q-J-10. If they were any weaker than that, the third round of diamonds would again promote a trump trick for West.

His mind made up, Soloway played the ace of clubs. His diamond continuation then doomed the contract to defeat. Blum did not know this yet and decided to ruff the third diamond with the king. By leading the queen of trumps next he could pick up the trump suit if East had started with a singleton nine. It was not to be. Both defenders followed low on the queen of trumps and a trick had to be lost to West's remaining jack-nine. The game was one down.

Louisa, who had not followed the play, looked closely at Blum. Such a dummy she gives him and he goes down? Perhaps, against these famous names, he had not given the play his full concentration. There was no excuse for that.

This match could be won!

The cards continued to run in the North-South direction and Blum's declarer play was tested on this board:

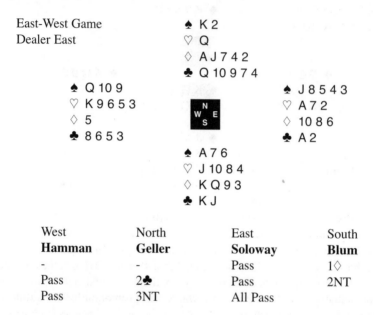

East-West Game
Dealer East

♠ K 2
♡ Q
◇ A J 7 4 2
♣ Q 10 9 7 4

♠ Q 10 9
♡ K 9 6 5 3
◇ 5
♣ 8 6 5 3

♠ J 8 5 4 3
♡ A 7 2
◇ 10 8 6
♣ A 2

♠ A 7 6
♡ J 10 8 4
◇ K Q 9 3
♣ K J

West	North	East	South
Hamman	**Geller**	**Soloway**	**Blum**
-	-	Pass	1◇
Pass	2♣	Pass	2NT
Pass	3NT	All Pass	

Hamman led the five of hearts to the queen and ace, Soloway returning the heart seven. Blum paused to consider his play to this trick. The most likely division of the heart suit was 5-3. Suppose he were to play the jack of hearts now. West would allow this to hold, retaining his K-9-6 over the 10-8. The contract would then go down if East held the ace of clubs and could lead a third round of hearts from his side.

Blum eventually pulled out the eight of hearts, spinning the card on to the baize. As the cards lay, the contract was now secure. West won with the nine, cashed the heart king and cleared the suit. When Blum eventually played on clubs it was East who produced the ace. He had no heart to play and nine tricks resulted.

Hamman nodded his enormous head. 'You took the right view in hearts,' he observed. 'If I hold the ace of clubs, you'd go down on that line.'

'With king fifth in hearts, the club ace and perhaps one of the spade honours, you might have bid,' Blum replied. 'That was the only clue I had.'

'The diamond game is easy,' Soloway observed. 'Just two aces to lose.'

Both sides performed competently on the next four or five boards. Blum then arrived in 3NT again.

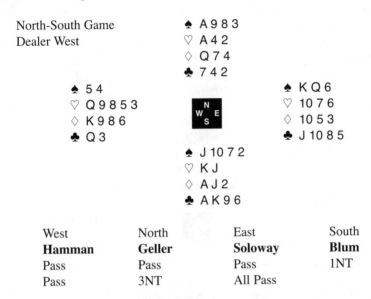

North-South Game
Dealer West

♠ A 9 8 3
♡ A 4 2
◇ Q 7 4
♣ 7 4 2

♠ 5 4
♡ Q 9 8 5 3
◇ K 9 8 6
♣ Q 3

♠ K Q 6
♡ 10 7 6
◇ 10 5 3
♣ J 10 8 5

♠ J 10 7 2
♡ K J
◇ A J 2
♣ A K 9 6

West	North	East	South
Hamman	**Geller**	**Soloway**	**Blum**
Pass	Pass	Pass	1NT
Pass	3NT	All Pass	

Blum opened a 15-17 point 1NT and Louisa raised directly to game in notrumps, not seeing any benefit to Stayman on her 4-3-3-3 shape. Hamman led the five of hearts and Blum won in hand with the jack. A spade to the nine lost to East's king and back came the ten of hearts, won with the king.

Blum paused for thought. What would happen if he took another spade finesse and it lost? East would clear the hearts and the contract would then depend on the diamond finesse. Perhaps he should play on diamonds first, attacking the potential entry to the danger hand. Yes, that looked best.

When Blum led a diamond towards dummy, Hamman had no winning option. If he rose with the king and cleared the hearts, his partner would have no heart to return when he came on lead in spades. Hamman chose to play low and dummy's queen of diamonds won the trick. Blum then returned to the club ace and ran the jack of spades. He was pleased to see this lose to the queen, since his careful play in diamonds would not have been needed if the other missing spade honour was onside. East returned his last heart but Blum claimed nine tricks and the game.

Hamman and Soloway exchanged a brief glance. It was annoying that the two tricky notrump contracts had fallen to the professional rather than the sponsor. Still, her time would come.

When scores were compared at the end of the first set the Nickell team had a lead of 5 IMPs.

'Not so good,' observed Louisa. 'I was hoping to take advantage of them having their sponsor playing.'

'We all played well, Louisa,' said Marty Bechman. 'Against that Kansas team we faced yesterday we'd be 30 IMPs up.'

'Against this team we need to play even better,' Louisa replied.

The second set brought Meckstroth and Rodwell to Louisa's table. She was immediately put to the test on this board:

```
Game All                    ♠ K J 9 7 6 4
Dealer South                ♡ 7 6 3
                            ◇ 8 5 4
                            ♣ 2
     ♠ 8 5                                      ♠ 10 3
     ♡ A 9 4              ┌─────────┐           ♡ Q J 10 5
     ◇ Q J 3             │    N     │           ◇ 10 9 7
     ♣ K J 8 5 3         │  W   E   │           ♣ Q 9 6 4
                         │    S     │
                          └─────────┘
                            ♠ A Q 2
                            ♡ K 8 2
                            ◇ A K 6 2
                            ♣ A 10 7
```

West	North	East	South
Rodwell	**Blum**	**Meckstroth**	**Geller**
-	-	-	2NT
Pass	3♡	Pass	3♠
Pass	4♠	All Pass	

Eric Rodwell, who was wearing a smart jacket and tie, led the five of trumps against the spade game. Louisa won in hand with the ace and led a second round of trumps to the jack, both defenders following. What next?

If diamonds were 3-3 and East held ◇3, she could arrange to lose a diamond trick to the safe West hand, setting up a winner for a heart discard. Yes, she thought, that was the best line. She would lead diamonds twice towards the closed hand, ducking if the three appeared from East. If instead West held four diamonds, the contract could be made by a loser-on-loser play – eliminating clubs and throwing a heart from dummy on the fourth round of diamonds; West would then be endplayed.

At Trick 3 Louisa led a diamond from dummy. When the seven appeared from East, rather than the hoped-for three, she won with the ace. Rodwell, who had a good idea of what was going on, ditched the diamond queen under the ace. After cashing ♣A, Louisa reached dummy with a club ruff and led another diamond. Once again the three-spot failed to appear from East. He contributed the nine and Louisa won with the king.

Rodwell could place his partner with the ten of diamonds, since with 9-7 doubleton he would have played high-low in the suit. Anxious to avoid being thrown in, he disposed of the jack of diamonds under declarer's king.

Louisa eliminated the clubs and, hoping for the best, led a third round of diamonds. It was not her lucky day. The suit broke 3-3 but East won the trick with the ten and fired the heart queen through the king. The defenders scored three heart tricks and the game was one down.

'Such a nice play, I made there,' Louisa declared. 'An avoidance play just like Terence Reese. East's diamonds were too good, unfortunately.'

Blum gave a small nod. She had played it OK, for her. Why not try a club towards her hand at Trick 3, though? If East happens to play low you can insert the ten and set up a discard for one of dummy's diamonds, subsequently ruffing the suit good. What if East put in a high club? Well, she would have to guess whether to continue with ♣10, playing West for the remaining two club honours, or to play on diamonds. Probably better to revert to diamonds in that case.

'There's no justice in this game,' continued Louisa. 'Declarer will probably go down at the other table, not having found my avoidance play, and there will be no swing.'

A few boards later, Louisa found herself under the spotlight again.

Game All

Dealer North

♠	K Q 4 2
♡	Q 2
◊	A J 8 5
♣	A Q 5

West:
♠ 9 8 6
♡ K J 9 8 4 3
◊ 7 3
♣ J 7

East:
♠ 7 5
♡ 10 7 6
◊ K 9 4
♣ K 10 8 6 4

South:
♠ A J 10 3
♡ A 5
◊ Q 10 6 2
♣ 9 3 2

West	North	East	South
Rodwell	**Blum**	**Meckstroth**	**Geller**
-	1◊	Pass	1♠
Pass	3♠	Pass	4♠
All Pass			

With six losers in his hand Blum would not have rebid any more than 3♠ even facing a professional partner. Louisa advanced to game and Rodwell led the nine of trumps. After drawing trumps in three rounds, Louisa ran the queen of diamonds to East's king.

When a heart was returned, she paused to consider her play to the trick. Was it possible that East had switched to a heart from the king when he had a safe exit in diamonds? In any case, what would happen if she rose with the ace of hearts and East did hold the king? The contract would be guaranteed! She could cash the remaining diamonds and exit with a heart. East would have to win and lead into the club tenace or give a ruff-and-discard. Yes, and it seemed the defenders might be in trouble even if West won the heart exit.

Louisa won with the heart ace, cashed the remaining diamonds and exited with a heart. West won and led the jack of clubs, covered by the queen and king. Louisa won East's club exit with the nine and the game had been made.

Meckstroth gave Louisa a friendly smile. 'Who's meant to be the professional here?' he asked.

'It wasn't very difficult,' Louisa replied. 'Just the sort of hand I like.'

When scores were compared for the second time, the Geller team found they had lost further ground. They were now 23 IMPs adrift.

'We must win the next set by at least 30 or 40 IMPs,' Louisa informed her team mates. 'It is the last time their sponsor will be playing.'

The three pros looked at each other. Win the next set by 30 or 40 IMPs? Is that all she wanted?

In the third set the two sponsors faced each other. Nick Nickell arrived in the first slam of the match.

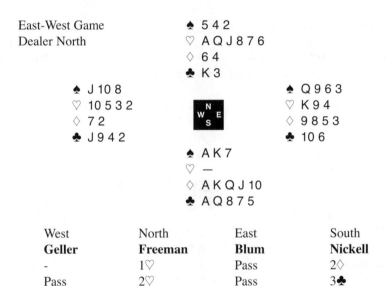

East-West Game
Dealer North

♠ 5 4 2
♡ A Q J 8 7 6
♢ 6 4
♣ K 3

♠ J 10 8
♡ 10 5 3 2
♢ 7 2
♣ J 9 4 2

♠ Q 9 6 3
♡ K 9 4
♢ 9 8 5 3
♣ 10 6

♠ A K 7
♡ —
♢ A K Q J 10
♣ A Q 8 7 5

West	North	East	South
Geller	**Freeman**	**Blum**	**Nickell**
-	1♡	Pass	2♢
Pass	2♡	Pass	3♣
Pass	3♡	Pass	6NT
All Pass			

Louisa led the jack of spades and Nickell won with the ace. He could count eleven top tricks and a 3-3 club break would bring the total to thirteen. Since he was only in a small slam, four club tricks would be sufficient. Nickell surveyed the dummy thoughtfully. He needed to cash the heart ace at some stage and could not afford to duck a club after the defenders' ♡K had been set up. How could this be arranged?

Declarer soon spotted the solution. He must duck the very first round of clubs. This would set up the suit provided it broke no worse than 4-2. It would also leave the king of clubs intact as an entry to cash dummy's ace of hearts.

When declarer ducked a club at Trick 2, Blum won in the East seat and returned a spade. Nickell produced the king and crossed to the king of clubs, both defenders following. 'They're all there now,' he said. 'I'll throw the spade loser on the heart ace and my hand is high.'

Louisa looked suspiciously at the declarer. The man calls himself a sponsor? How could he find a play like ducking the first club? 'Is it any better if I lead a heart?' she enquired. 'That sets up the king before you can get the clubs going.'

'It depends on what your partner returns when he wins with the king of hearts,' Nickell replied. 'If he plays anything except a club, my fifth diamond will squeeze you in the round suits.'

Blum nodded respectfully in Nickell's direction. He was right. A club return would deal a fatal blow to declarer's entry situation. Perhaps after this exchange Louisa would at last realise what a task it was to beat such a team over 64 boards.

Later in the set Nickell arrived in another slam. This was the lay-out:

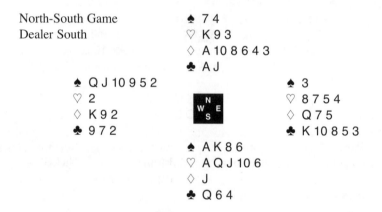

```
North-South Game          ♠ 7 4
Dealer South              ♡ K 9 3
                          ◇ A 10 8 6 4 3
                          ♣ A J
        ♠ Q J 10 9 5 2                    ♠ 3
        ♡ 2                               ♡ 8 7 5 4
        ◇ K 9 2            N              ◇ Q 7 5
        ♣ 9 7 2         W     E           ♣ K 10 8 5 3
                           S
                          ♠ A K 8 6
                          ♡ A Q J 10 6
                          ◇ J
                          ♣ Q 6 4
```

West	North	East	South
Geller	**Freeman**	**Blum**	**Nickell**
-	-	-	1♡
2♠	3◇	Pass	3NT
Pass	4♡	Pass	4♠
Pass	6♡	All Pass	

Louisa led the queen of spades against the slam and Nickell won with the ace. It was by no means obvious how to play the hand. One option was to play on the diamond suit. Another possibility was to cross to the ace of diamonds and lead a spade towards his hand. If East chose to ruff, however, and the club king was offside, it would still be necessary to set up the diamonds.

Nickell drew two rounds of trumps with the ace and queen, West following once and then throwing a spade. His next move was to lead the jack of diamonds. Louisa declined to cover and declarer now had to calculate whether to play dummy's ace. Suppose he did and the play continued: diamond ruff, king of trumps, diamond ruff. East would then have a long trump and the only way to reach the good diamonds (assuming they had broken 3-3) would be a club to the ace, exposing a second loser. That was no good.

Nickell decided to run the jack of diamonds. Blum won with the queen and surveyed the scene unhappily. If he returned a trump, declarer would win with dummy's bare king, ruff the diamonds good and draw trumps. He could then cross to the ace of clubs and claim the remainder. The only hope for the defence, a slender one, was that Louisa held the club queen. Blum switched boldly to a club, taking his only chance, but the play brought no dividend. The trick was won by dummy's jack and declarer soon had twelve tricks before him.

Louisa returned her cards resignedly to the wallet. 'It is any better if I cover the diamond?' she asked.

'I don't think so,' Nickell replied. 'I win with the ace and ruff a diamond. Trump to the king and I can duck the third round of diamonds to your partner's queen.'

'That's right,' said Blum. 'I can't attack the club entry from my side.'

With one set to go, the Nickell team led by 46 IMPs. The pros on the Geller team knew that Louisa would not entertain any thoughts of a concession. They would not have suggested such an action even if they had been 70 IMPs behind.

Blum and Louisa took their seats to face Hamman and Soloway for the final set of sixteen boards. First to speak, at favourable vulnerability, Blum looked down at this moderate hand:

♠ K 10 9 8 4
♡ 9 6 5
♢ 9 8 6 4
♣ 2

They weren't going to pick up 46 IMPs by sitting passively, waiting for this team to make mistakes. He would have to generate some action. Blum reached into his bidding box and opened Two Spades – a weak two.

Hamman passed and Louisa sat for quite a while considering her response. Just my luck to find her with a good hand, thought Blum. Surely she would make some allowance for the match situation and the current vulnerability. If they went over the top on this one, there would surely be no way back.

Blum watched nervously as Louisa grabbed a handful of cards from her bidding box. She had bid Six Spades!

There was no further bidding and it was Bob Hamman to lead. 'How do you play your weak twos?' he asked.

'They can be very weak in third seat,' Louisa replied. 'He should have a sound weak two in the first seat. I hope so, anyway.'

Hamman led the king of clubs and down went the dummy. This was the full deal:

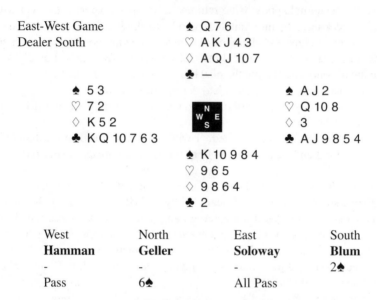

East-West Game	♠ Q 7 6
Dealer South	♡ A K J 4 3
	♢ A Q J 10 7
	♣ —

♠ 5 3   ♠ A J 2
♡ 7 2   ♡ Q 10 8
♢ K 5 2   ♢ 3
♣ K Q 10 7 6 3   ♣ A J 9 8 5 4

♠ K 10 9 8 4
♡ 9 6 5
♢ 9 8 6 4
♣ 2

West	North	East	South
Hamman	**Geller**	**Soloway**	**Blum**
-	-	-	2♠
Pass	6♠	All Pass	

Blum surveyed the dummy, his worst fears confirmed. The ace of trumps was missing and there were potential further losers in spades, hearts and diamonds. What was the point of leaping to six on a hand like that? Why not respond 2NT to find out more about his hand?

Desperately short of entries to the South hand, Blum ruffed the opening lead with dummy's queen. He then led a low trump, inserting the ten when East played low. He was over the first hurdle when the ten won the trick. Blum now cast an eye on his red-suit holdings. Five heart tricks would be no use to him, since he would still have to take the diamond finesse. It was better to play on diamonds, since five diamond tricks would allow him to dispose of the potential loser in hearts.

At Trick 3 Blum led a diamond to the queen. Again his luck held and the queen won the trick. When he led a second round of trumps, East rose with the ace and exited safely with jack of trumps. Blum won with the king and repeated the diamond finesse. Almost apologetically, he then claimed twelve tricks.

'Not the best lead, sorry,' said Hamman. 'A trump or a heart lead beats it easily.'

From Blum's point of view, there was depressingly little action on the next string of boards. They might gain the odd IMP or two but unless Marty and Larry had struck gold at the other table prospects of overcoming the 46-IMP lead were bleak.

Blum re-focussed his attention as he sorted his cards for the next board and found that he had a very big hand. Perhaps, somehow, he could generate a swing.

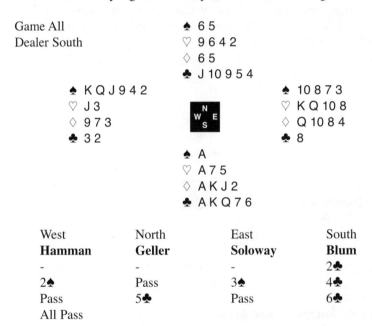

West	North	East	South
Hamman	**Geller**	**Soloway**	**Blum**
-	-	-	2♣
2♠	Pass	3♠	4♣
Pass	5♣	Pass	6♣
All Pass			

Blum had little idea of his partner's hand at the time he had to make his final decision. Hoping that Louisa would hold something of value in the red suits, he ventured a sixth club. There was no further bidding and the king of spades was led.

Blum surveyed Louisa's dummy impassively. Almost nothing for him! Against weak opposition he could cash the ace of hearts early in the play and eliminate the other suits. If a defender had started with king doubleton of hearts and failed to unblock the king under the ace, he could be thrown in and would have to concede a ruff-and-discard. Bermuda Bowl winners were scarcely likely to miss a technical defence like that. What else could he try?

If East held the length in both red suits, including the queen of diamonds, it would be possible to squeeze him. Yes, that was a better shot. Blum drew trumps with the ace and king. He was pleased to see West turn up with two trumps, since this increased the chance that East would be long in the red suits. Blum next led a low heart from his hand. The purpose of this was two-fold. It would rectify the count, preparing for a squeeze, and with any luck it would also isolate the heart guard with East. West rose with the jack of hearts and East overtook with the queen, switching to the eight of diamonds.

Blum was committed to his line of play. He inserted the jack of diamonds and breathed more freely when this won the trick. A low trump to the jack allowed him to ruff dummy's remaining spade with the queen. He then cashed the ace of hearts and returned to dummy with the trump ten. These cards remained:

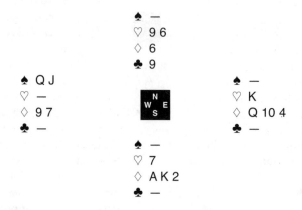

'Play the last trump,' said Blum.

East was caught in a simple squeeze. Since he had to keep the king of hearts to guard against the dummy's nine, he discarded a diamond. Blum then scored three more tricks in the diamond suit and the slam was home.

'I didn't have much for you,' Louisa observed.

'No,' replied Blum, with an amused shake of the head. 'We were lucky to make it.'

Blum and Louisa picked up potentially useful plus scores on the next three boards and the match drew to a close. Hamman and Soloway departed and Geller looked excitedly across the table at Blum. 'Such a set we have had!' she exclaimed. 'If Larry and Marty have done well too, we may have won it.'

Once in a while miracles do happen and Louisa became increasingly excited as the minutes ticked by. Eventually she spotted her other pair returning. 'Jerry!' she said. 'They are coming.'

Louisa peered anxiously at her two team mates as they made their way towards her. The signs were not good. Bechman was shaking his head. Surely they hadn't had a poor set, thought Louisa. Not just at this moment, please God, when her own card was so good.

'Sorry, folks,' said Larry Smith, who was first to reach the table. 'We pushed too hard on an early board and had another bad one later. No good, I'm afraid.'

Louisa flopped back into her chair. 'Jerry and I, we have played like world champions in the last set,' she declared. 'We thought we were certain to win.'

'Sorry, Louisa,' said Marty Bechman. 'We tried our best, believe me.'

Nickell had extended his lead to 55 IMPs and the Geller team's adventures in the Spingold were over for another year. Louisa was still shaking her head in disbelief. 'Jerry and I made two wonderful slams,' she continued. 'Wonderful slams, they were. I felt sure it would be enough.'

'You played very well, Louisa,' Bechman declared. 'Against any other team it would have been enough to win.'

Louisa looked at the disconsolate faces around her. She was the captain and at moments like this it was her job to help the team to recover its spirits. 'Well, boys, it has been a day for us all to treasure,' she said, rising to her feet. 'Come on, let's cheer ourselves up with a late-night meal and a drink.'

Louisa shepherded her team-mates towards the hotel's Beni-Haha restaurant. 'Just what I need,' she said, as she took her seat and studied the menu. 'I always sleep well after a plateful of raw fish!'

7
Jerry Blum's Last Chance

During his three decades as a bridge pro, Blum had played opposite all manner of partners. Most of them were pleasant enough, with no great pretensions about their own abilities at the game. A small handful were downright unpleasant, treating the pro as some sort of hired servant. It made little difference to Blum. If he could slip two hundred or so into his pocket at the end of the session, that was good enough for him. If he happened to enjoy the game too... well, that was a bonus.

On the present occasion he was about to partner one of his least favourite partners. Dan Lerner had made a tidy sum selling refrigerators and had been one of the best in the business, as he never tired of telling everyone. When it came to bridge, he regarded himself as a very sound performer. If the finishing position was not to his liking he was usually quick to blame the pro.

'Ah, Jerry, how you doin'?' called Lerner, arriving at the Pompano Club in Fort Lauderdale. 'Long time no see.'

'I'm great, thanks,' Blum replied. 'And you?'

'Just back from three weeks in Hawaii,' said Lerner. 'You know what the girls are like over there. Couldn't keep them off me.'

Blum smiled politely. Why any girl should voluntarily approach within a hundred yards of Lerner was a mystery. Unless he was waving his cheque-book around.

An early round of the pairs saw Blum and his partner facing student opposition. It as a mid-semester Tuesday afternoon and he wondered why the denim-clad duo weren't at their studies. Ah well, that was their business.

Lerner reached a slam on the first board of the round:

Love All
Dealer South

	♠ 10 7 6 5 2	
	♡ 9 5	
	◇ A Q	
	♣ A 8 7 5	

♠ —		♠ K 9 8 3
♡ Q 10 7 4 3	**N**	♡ J 8 6
◇ 10 8 5 2	**W E**	◇ 6 4 3
♣ J 9 6 4	**S**	♣ K 10 2

	♠ A Q J 4	
	♡ A K 2	
	◇ K J 9 7	
	♣ Q 3	

West	North	East	South
Steve	**Jerry**	**John**	**Dan**
Maggs	**Blum**	**Wittes**	**Lerner**
-	-	-	2NT
Pass	3♡	Pass	4♠
Pass	6♠	All Pass	

When Lerner broke the transfer response, Blum decided to keep the bidding simple and jump to a small slam. A cue-bidding sequence might help the defenders to find a heart lead. After any other lead, one or more of dummy's hearts might vanish on any surplus diamond winners declarer held.

A low diamond was led and Lerner surveyed the dummy with mixed feelings. There was little chance of avoiding a club loser, so it seemed he would need to find the king of trumps onside. He certainly had his break of the transfer, with four good trumps and a ruffing value. If the slam went down, he would blame it on Blum's jump to the six level on five small trumps. 'Play the ace,' said Lerner.

A trump to the queen brought good news and bad news. The finesse won but West showed out. How could he now avoid two losers in the black suits?

Lerner cashed two top hearts and ruffed a heart. He then played dummy's queen of diamonds and took a second trump finesse. The ace of trumps was followed by the king of diamonds, leaving these cards out:

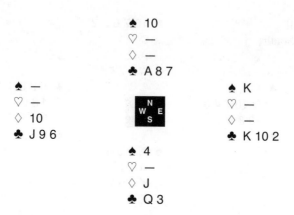

When Lerner played his last diamond winner, the student in the East seat saw that he would be endplayed if he ruffed. He discarded a club instead, but this only delayed his fate. When Lerner exited with a trump, East had to lead away from the king of clubs. Twelve tricks resulted.

'Make a note of the hand, Jerry!' Lerner exclaimed. 'You can use it in that book you're writing.'

'Maybe I will,' Blum replied.

'Put it in the chapter on end-plays,' continued Lerner. 'Or perhaps in some chapter on reading the cards.'

Blum did want to embarrass his client but if he used the deal at all it would be in a chapter called 'Safety Plays Within a Single Suit'. If Lerner had led the ten on the first round of trumps he could have picked up the suit without loss. No endplay would have been needed and he could have made the slam whoever held the king of clubs.

Lerner smiled to himself as he returned his cards to the wallet. If these boys knew there was a professional at the table, they would probably think it was him. Blum hadn't done anything to justify his two-fifty so far. Pros were thick on the ground in Florida. If Blum didn't wake his ideas up, he would maybe give one of the other guys a chance.

This was the second board of the round:

East-West Game
Dealer East

♠ A 3
♡ A Q 9
◇ J 7
♣ A 10 9 7 5 4

♠ Q 9 6 4
♡ K 4 2
◇ 10 9 8 3
♣ 8 6

♠ 8 7 5
♡ 5 3
◇ A 6 5 4 2
♣ Q J 3

♠ K J 10 2
♡ J 10 8 7 6
◇ K Q
♣ K 2

West	North	East	South
Steve	**Jerry**	**John**	**Dan**
Maggs	**Blum**	**Wittes**	**Lerner**
-	-	Pass	1♡
Pass	2♣	Pass	2NT
Pass	3♡	Pass	4♡
Pass	6♡	All Pass	

Blum was not quite worth his leap to 6♡ but it was his policy to keep the bidding simple when playing with a client. West led the ten of diamonds and down went the dummy.

'Not much there for me,' Lerner observed, shaking his head. If the slam went down, it certainly wouldn't be his fault. Was he laying out a full two-fifty just for someone to overbid wildly on every hand?

East won the first trick with the diamond ace and returned ♠8. Lerner's jack was covered by the queen and dummy's ace won the trick. After a diamond to the king Lerner ran the jack of trumps. He perked up when this won the trick. Perhaps the slam could be made after all. Both defenders followed when a trump was played to the queen but the king of trumps refused to show.

Lerner paused to plan the remainder of the play. What could he do with his remaining loser in the spade suit? He couldn't ruff it with dummy's ace or West would make a trick with the trump king. No, it seemed that he would have to set up the club suit. West would need to hold three clubs for this to be possible. Was there any law against that?

Lerner cashed the king and ace of clubs, all following, and continued with a third round of the suit. He muttered some inaudible swearword when it was East who produced the club queen. West overruffed declarer's ten of trumps with the king and the slam was one down.

'I had my bid, Jerry,' Lerner complained. 'I don't know why you leapt to six like that. It was a poor slam.'

'Yeah, sorry, I should have just made a try,' Blum replied, as he reached for the scoresheet.

'Make a try and I sign off,' Lerner continued. 'I wouldn't go to slam with a pile of kings and jacks.'

The student in the West seat leaned forward to look at the other scores on the board. 'They all made twelve tricks,' he informed his partner.

His partner nodded. 'My spade switch gave him a chance to go wrong,' he replied. 'If he wins in the South hand with the king, he can draw trumps, ruff the clubs good and use the spade ace as an entry.'

Blum would not have pointed this out himself but it was music to his ears to hear the opponents doing so.

'Easy to miss, though,' he said. 'Bad luck, Dan.'

On the next round Lerner and Blum sat East-West against a retired married couple who were regulars at the club. This was the first deal they played:

Love All	♠ Q 6 3
Dealer South	♡ K 6 2
	◇ 10 9 7 4 3
	♣ 8 6

♠ K J 10 8	♠ 9 5
♡ Q J 10 8 5	♡ 9 7 4 3
◇ A 5	◇ 8 6
♣ A 4	♣ 10 9 7 5 2

♠ A 7 4 2
♡ A
◇ K Q J 2
♣ K Q J 3

West	North	East	South
Dan	**George**	**Jerry**	**Margie**
Lerner	**Tyler**	**Blum**	**Tyler**
-	-	-	1◇
1♡	3◇	Pass	5◇
All Pass			

George Tyler, who was wearing a chequered shirt more appropriate for line dancing than playing bridge, leaned forward. 'Before you lead,' he said, in a mid-West accent, 'I should tell you that my 3◊ bid was a jump pre-empt.'

'So it was,' said his grey-haired wife. 'I'm afraid I forgot or I would have alerted it. If George held eleven points he would have made a bid in your suit instead. What was it, hearts or spades?'

'I bid a heart,' said Lerner.

'Yes, well in that case he would come 2♡ with a good hand,' Margie Tyler continued. '3◊ is a jump pre-empt.'

Lerner led the queen of hearts and declarer won with the ace. She was disappointed to see that there were three apparent losers on the horizon, despite her fine 20-count. Ah well, she would have to draw trumps and see what happened.

At Trick 2 Margie Tyler led the two of trumps from her hand. Not sensing any danger, Lerner followed with the five. Dummy's ten won the trick and declarer proceeded to cash the king of hearts, throwing a spade. She then ruffed dummy's last heart and played a second round of trumps to West's ace, the suit dividing 2-2.

Somewhat late, Lerner paused for thought. A spade exit was surely no good; declarer was marked with the ace and the queen was visible in the dummy. A low club could hardly be right because he would be endplayed again on the second round of clubs. No, he would have to hope for the best and play ace and another club.

When Lerner followed this course, Margie Tyler smiled brightly and faced her hand. 'Dummy's two spade losers go on my clubs,' she said.

Blum nodded. 'You should take the first round of trumps, Dan,' he said. 'You can exit safely in a red suit and make a spade trick later.'

'Easy to say that now but you might have held a singleton trump honour,' Lerner replied. 'In any case, they had a double heart stopper. 3NT is easy.'

George Tyler was inspecting the scoresheet. 'It can't be as easy as all that,' he said. 'Everyone in 3NT went down. I think you'll find the defenders score three hearts and two aces.'

Margie Tyler smiled lovingly at her husband. 'If I'd remembered that your 3◊ was a jump pre-empt I would have bid 3NT!' she said. 'It was a lucky one for us.'

Halfway through the afternoon Dan Lerner found himself playing a slam contract.

Game All   ♠ A K 6 3
Dealer East   ♡ K Q 8 2
                     ♢ 6 5
                     ♣ A 6 3

♠ Q 9 4		♠ J 10 7 2
♡ 5	N	♡ 7 6 4
♢ K 10 9 8 3	W E	♢ 4
♣ K J 8 5	S	♣ Q 10 9 7 2

                     ♠ 8 5
                     ♡ A J 10 9 3
                     ♢ A Q J 7 2
                     ♣ 4

West	North	East	South
Connie	**Jerry**	**Mary**	**Dan**
Lagrange	**Blum**	**Wallace**	**Lerner**
-	-	Pass	1♡
Pass	1♠	Pass	2♢
Pass	3♣	Pass	3♢
Pass	4NT	Pass	5♡
Pass	6♡	All Pass	

Blum would have looked for a grand slam in normal circumstances, bidding 5NT to tell his partner that all the key cards were present. It wasn't worth it, playing at club level where you normally scored well for making a small slam. In any case Lerner was not the world's best dummy player.

Connie Lagrange, who was wearing a small black dress that would have suited someone half her age, led a trump against the slam. Lerner won in hand and drew trumps in two more rounds, ending in dummy. A diamond to the queen lost to West's king and when diamonds proved to be 5-1 there was no way to avoid going one down.

'It was a good slam,' said Lerner. 'Diamonds 4-2 or 5-1 onside and there's no problem.'

Connie Lagrange looked happily at her partner. 'I had king-ten-nine fifth in diamonds,' she said. 'That's why we got him down.'

'Well played, Connie,' her partner replied.

'It's no good taking the diamond finesse before drawing trumps,' continued Lerner. 'East gets a diamond ruff then.'

Blum nodded. He had no wish to embarrass his client, particularly in front of two ladies, but the contract should have been made. The best line was to cash the ace of diamonds, then cross to the club ace and lead a second round of diamonds towards the South hand. If East ruffed a loser, he could win the return and draw trumps in one more round, subsequently taking a ruffing finesse in diamonds. There would still be a spare trump in dummy to ruff the last diamond. If instead East declined to ruff the second diamond, it would be easy to ruff two diamonds with high trumps.

Nothing I could do,' said Lerner, as he extracted his cards for the next deal. Blum did likewise, picking up this collection:

$$\spadesuit\ 9\ 8\ 7\ 5$$
$$\heartsuit\ A\ Q\ 6\ 4$$
$$\diamondsuit\ -$$
$$\clubsuit\ K\ Q\ 10\ 4\ 2$$

With the score at Love All, he opened 1♣ and heard Lerner reply 1♠. How strongly should he rebid? There were only five losers in his hand but the trumps were poor and he had a minimum point-count. Best to hold back a bit, particularly since Lerner would be playing the contract. Blum rebid just 2♠ and said no more when Lerner raised to the spade game. This was the full deal:

Love All
Dealer North

```
                    ♠ 9 8 7 5
                    ♡ A Q 6 4
                    ◇ —
                    ♣ K Q 10 4 2
♠ 3                                    ♠ Q J 10 6
♡ 10 5 3 2          N                  ♡ K J 9
◇ A Q J 8 2       W   E                ◇ 9 5 4 3
♣ 9 8 6             S                  ♣ 7 5
                    ♠ A K 4 2
                    ♡ 8 7
                    ◇ K 10 7 6
                    ♣ A J 3
```

West	North	East	South
Connie	**Jerry**	**Mary**	**Dan**
Lagrange	**Blum**	**Wallace**	**Lerner**
-	1♣	Pass	1♠
Pass	2♠	Pass	4♠
All Pass			

The eight of clubs was led and Lerner cast his usual critical eye over Blum's dummy. How many tricks was he likely to lose? One trump, if they broke 3-2, and that might be all if the heart finesse was right. 'That's a bit good, Jerry,' he said. 'I'd have bid 4◊, splinter bid, on your hand.'

Lerner won the club lead with the jack and drew two rounds of trumps, pleased to see the 4-1 break. Good! Eleven tricks would be the limit for anyone in a slam. When he turned his attention to the club suit, the smartly dressed lady in the East seat ruffed the third round and drew a further round of trumps. She exited with a diamond and Lerner tried his luck with the king, covered by West's ace. After ruffing in the dummy, Lerner found that he only had nine tricks at his disposal. A successful heart finesse would bump this to ten but, somewhat embarrassingly, he now had no entry to his hand.

Lerner sat back in his chair, shaking his head. Perhaps he should have taken the heart finesse before playing on clubs. If it had lost, though, East would have been able to draw all the trumps before switching to diamonds.

Lerner conceded one down, having to lead hearts from the dummy. 'The heart finesse was wrong anyway,' he said. 'It didn't matter what I did.'

The white-haired Connie Lagrange knew Lerner well. 'Just as well your partner didn't bid more strongly,' she reprimanded him. 'You'd have gone to a slam with your 15-count.'

Mary Wallace turned towards Blum. 'Could the game have been made, Mr Blum?' she asked.

'Yes, at IMPs Dan would have played it differently,' Blum replied. 'He would cash just one high trump and then play on clubs. You can ruff and play a trump back to declarer's king but now the cross-ruff is set up. Declarer loses just two trumps and a heart.'

'That's not the right line at Pairs,' said Lerner. 'When trumps are 3-2 the defender with the doubleton trump might ruff the third club. I'd lose the overtrick then.'

The two ladies exchanged a glance. It was obvious to everyone at the table that Lerner would have played exactly the same way at any form of the game. 'Ah yes, you'd lose the overtrick,' said Connie Lagrange.

With three rounds to go, Blum estimated their score at a modest 55%. Lerner had inflated ideas of his own abilities at the game and would doubtless view such a score with disappointment. Perhaps they could pick up some good results on this round. Not that he recognised the middle-aged opponents who were awaiting them.

```
Game All                  ♠ A Q 10 7 6
Dealer South              ♡ A 6
                          ◊ K 6 3 2
                          ♣ K 7
       ♠ 2                                    ♠ 4
       ♡ K Q J 9          ┌─────┐            ♡ 10 8 7 5 3 2
       ◊ A J 8 5          │  N  │            ◊ 7
       ♣ Q J 10 6         │W   E│            ♣ 9 8 5 4 2
                          │  S  │
                          └─────┘
                          ♠ K J 9 8 5 3
                          ♡ 4
                          ◊ Q 10 9 4
                          ♣ A 3
```

West	North	East	South
Jerry	**Norman**	**Dan**	**Johnny**
Blum	**Grey**	**Lerner**	**Carmichael**
-	-	-	1♠
Dble	4NT	Pass	5♡
Pass	6♠	All Pass	

Blum led the king of hearts and down went the dummy. 'Don't know if this guy's foolin' around with the double,' the North player declared. 'Seemed like an obvious Blackwood bid anyway.'

Blum smiled to himself. He didn't know them and they obviously didn't know him. Would he psyche a vulnerable take-out double? With a client as a partner, what's more? It wasn't likely.

Johnny Carmichael peered at the dummy through his thick-lensed spectacles. 'Win with the ace,' he said.

Lerner signalled with the eight of hearts to show an even number of cards in the suit. Declarer couldn't hold a singleton heart, could he, thought Blum. That would be unlucky.

Carmichael drew a round of trumps and ruffed a heart in his hand, much to Blum's disappointment. He then played the ace and king of clubs, eliminating that suit. The lead was in dummy in this end position:

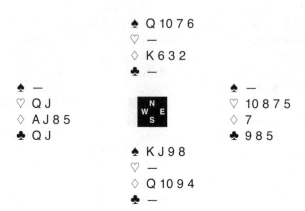

♠ Q 10 7 6
♡ —
◇ K 6 3 2
♣ —

♠ —
♡ Q J
◇ A J 8 5
♣ Q J

♠ —
♡ 10 8 7 5
◇ 7
♣ 9 8 5

♠ K J 9 8
♡ —
◇ Q 10 9 4
♣ —

Carmichael's next move was a diamond to the queen. Blum did not rush with his play to the trick. What was the shape of the South hand? Dan had shown an odd number of clubs. If declarer had started with 6-1-2-4 shape the slam was cold. It was more likely that South's initial shape had been 6-1-4-2. Yes, and in that case it would cost the contract to capture the queen of diamonds. He would be endplayed! If he exited with ◇5 declarer could win with dummy's ◇6. He would then re-enter his hand with a trump to run the ten of diamonds through the jack.

Pleased that he taken the trouble to count the hand, Blum allowed South's queen of diamonds to win. Declarer next led the nine of diamonds, hoping to slip the card past West. His luck was out. Blum covered with the jack, forcing dummy's king, and was then certain to score two diamond tricks. The slam was one down.

Blum modestly returned his cards to the wallet. Had Dan noticed the play in diamonds? Not that it would be within his repertoire to pass any compliment on the matter.

'Lead the ace of diamonds and I get a ruff,' said Lerner. 'We're lucky it went down after your heart lead.'

Carmichael turned his thick lenses in Lerner's direction. 'A heart lead was obvious from your partner's hand,' he informed him. 'He defended very well at the end, ducking the queen of diamonds.'

Lerner was unaccustomed to such reprimands. 'Yes, yes, ducking the queen, I saw,' he replied. 'It was a good defence.'

In the last round Blum and Lerner faced one of the characters of the club, Sam Reichardt. Blind for forty years since a motor bike crash after a friend's twenty-first birthday party, he played bridge of a moderate standard. Whenever he turned up to play, the club used Braille playing cards.

'Hi, Sam,' said Blum, taking the South seat. 'Making you move today, are they?'

'Howell movement, Jerry, yes,' Reichardt replied. 'No problem, though, with Joyce to steer me around.'

Blum turned towards Joyce Reichardt, who was neatly dressed in a blue two-piece. 'Has Sam been behaving himself?' he asked.

Joyce laughed. 'He likes to overbid, as you know,' she replied. 'We'd both be lifemasters by now if only he'd bid properly.'

'I'd rather enjoy the game than be a lifemaster,' Reichardt declared.

This was the first deal they played:

East-West Game
Dealer South

```
                    ♠ 10 2
                    ♡ K Q 2
                    ◇ A 6 5 4 2
                    ♣ K 7 4
  ♠ 9 4                          ♠ K Q J 5
  ♡ J 9 7 5 3        N           ♡ A 10
  ◇ 10 9 8         W   E         ◇ Q J 7 3
  ♣ 10 8 2           S           ♣ 9 6 5
                    ♠ A 8 7 6 3
                    ♡ 8 6 4
                    ◇ K
                    ♣ A Q J 3
```

West	North	East	South
Joyce	**Dan**	**Sam**	**Jerry**
Reichardt	**Lerner**	**Reichardt**	**Blum**
-	-	-	1♠
Pass	2◇	Pass	2♠
Pass	3♠	Pass	4♠
All Pass			

Blum arrived in a spade game and it was Joyce Reichardt to lead. 'I lead the ten of diamonds, Sam,' she said.

Lerner displayed his dummy. 'I put you with six spades for the rebid, Jerry,' he said. 'Three Spades is the bid you wanted on this, isn't it?'

'Er, yes,' Blum replied.

'Could have rebid 2NT, I suppose,' continued Lerner, 'but if you thought you'd already shown six spades, you might...'

'I'm so sorry to interrupt,' said Joyce Reichardt, 'but would you mind calling the dummy for Sam?'

'Ah yes, of course,' said Lerner. 'Sorry, Sam, I wasn't thinking.'

Lerner called out the thirteen cards in the dummy and play continued. Every time declarer played a card from the his own hand or the dummy he called out the card, for Sam's benefit. So did Sam's wife when she played a card in defence.

Blum won the diamond lead with the bare king and turned his mind to how he might restrict his trump losers to two. This would be a simple task if trumps were 3-3, of course. Was there any chance against a 4-2 break?

It seemed to Blum that he might survive if West held any doubleton that included the nine. At Trick 2 he led the six of trumps from his hand, running the card when West played low. Sam won with the jack of trumps and returned the queen of diamonds to dummy's ace. Blum discarded a heart from his hand and led the ten of trumps from dummy, intending to run it.

Sam fingered through his cards for a moment, sensing the Braille dots. Eventually he covered the ten of trumps with the king. Blum won with the ace and the nine fell from West. So far, so good. What next?

Blum could see that he was in danger of losing control if he simply knocked out East's remaining high trump. He would be forced in diamonds before he established the heart trick that he needed.

Blum decided to play a heart instead. Dummy's king lost to the ace and Sam returned another diamond, reducing declarer's trumps. It was still not safe to play a trump, since East could force declarer's last trump with the diamond jack. He would then score three trump tricks and the heart ace, defeating the game.

Blum crossed to the queen of hearts and ruffed a diamond, setting up a long card in the suit. He then cashed the ace and king of clubs, leaving these cards still to be played:

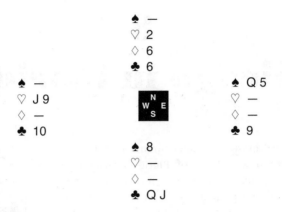

```
              ♠ —
              ♡ 2
              ◇ 6
              ♣ 6
♠ —                        ♠ Q 5
♡ J 9          N           ♡ —
◇ —         W     E        ◇ —
♣ 10           S           ♣ 9
              ♠ 8
              ♡ —
              ◇ —
              ♣ Q J
```

East's two trump tricks were about to be condensed into one. 'Play the diamond,' said Blum.

Sam Reichardt had no answer to this card. If he discarded a club Blum would do the same and then promote his last trump by leading a heart from dummy. Reichardt in fact chose to ruff low. Blum overruffed and scored the queen of clubs for his tenth trick. The game had been made.

'With anyone else as declarer, I would have doubled!' Reichardt informed his wife. 'I still don't know how he made it with the trumps breaking like that.'

'You helped him to set up that diamond,' Joyce replied.

'No, it's easy for me if you don't keep on playing diamonds,' said Blum. 'I can just draw trumps.'

Lerner entered the result on the travelling scoresheet, happy to see that it was a top. 'The notrump game has gone down most of the time,' he observed. 'They must have missed my raise on ten-one of spades.'

'A diamond lead would beat 3NT,' Blum replied. 'On a passive club lead, they would need to find the play I used in the spade suit.'

'Most hands are decided in the bidding,' Lerner continued. 'You're not writing a book on bidding, are you, Jerry? I'll write my hand down for you, in case you want to use it.'

Blum forced himself to nod politely. 'That's kind of you,' he replied.

Lerner smiled to himself as he wrote the hand down on the back of one of his business cards. 'The way things have gone in this session,' he said, 'you should be paying me!'

8
Chicago in Florida

Once a month during the winter Blum was invited to play Chicago with three of Florida's wealthiest residents. The game took place in Sol Steiner's sprawling ranch-style property in Boca Raton, only a half-hour drive from Blum's own place in West Palm Beach. The stakes of a dollar a point ($100 a hundred) were peanuts to the three millionaires. To Blum they represented a considerable, almost frightening, amount.
He was the best player, of course, and generally made a fair profit from such encounters. It was hard work, though. It could also be very stressful when a small fortune hung on one bid or one play from an inexperienced partner.

'I had to fire the new swimmin' pool guy,' said Sol Steiner, tapping the ash off his Lambert & Butler. 'Hadn't been here an hour before he was gone.'

'Ain't no-one willin' to work hard nowadays,' replied Henry Bendig, a tall man with a trim grey beard. 'Surprised he didn't make an effort on his first day.'

'That wasn't the problem,' Steiner continued. 'He was too damned good lookin'. Couldn't trust Marilyn if she caught an eyeful of that. I told the agency to send someone older.'

Steiner poured each player a good measure of bourbon and they moved to his oak-panelled gaming room. Blum drew Steiner in the cut for partners and the first chukker began.

Love All
Dealer North

	♠ A	
	♡ A J 7 6 3 2	
	◇ Q 6 2	
	♣ K 8 6	

♠ K J 9 6		♠ Q 8 4 2
♡ 10 8	N W E S	♡ K Q 9 5
◇ 8 7 4		◇ 9 3
♣ Q 10 9 2		♣ J 7 5

	♠ 10 7 5 3	
	♡ 4	
	◇ A K J 10 5	
	♣ A 4 3	

West	North	East	South
Henry	**Sol**	**Ronnie**	**Jerry**
Bendig	**Steiner**	**Neuman**	**Blum**
-	1♡	Pass	2◇
Pass	3♡	Pass	3NT
Pass	4◇	Pass	6◇
All Pass			

Bendig led the eight of trumps and down went the dummy. 'Only fourteen points,' Steiner observed. 'Nice shape, though.'

Blum paused to assess his prospects. Even though he was a hardened bridge pro and had played many times in this high-stake game, he still found it alarming that a non-vulnerable small slam was worth almost a thousand dollars. There was little point in ruffing two spades. That would bring the total to only eleven tricks and he would still need to establish dummy's heart suit. A better idea was to aim for one spade ruff and three tricks from the heart suit.

Blum won the trump lead in his hand and crossed to the ace of spades. Ace of hearts and a heart ruff returned the lead to the South hand and he ruffed a spade low. It was not possible to ruff three hearts in his hand, so he could survive a 4-2 heart break only by ducking a heart at some stage. The right moment was surely now, while dummy still had a trump left to deal with a spade return.

Blum led a low heart from dummy and discarded a spade from his hand. Ronnie Neuman won the trick in the East seat and returned a trump to the table's bare queen. Blum was then able to ruff a heart, setting up the suit. After drawing West's last trump, he claimed the contract.

Steiner nodded happily as he opened a new pack of Lambert & Butler king size. 'Some players would rebid just Two Hearts on my hand,' he said. 'When you've played the game as long as I have, you know when it is right to overbid.'

A couple of deals later, Blum arrived in a borderline spade game.

North-South Game
Dealer South

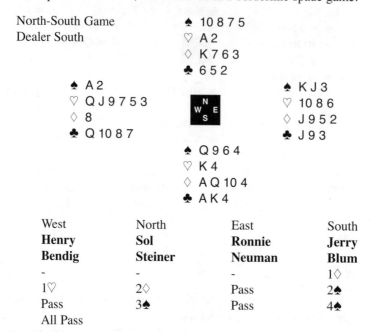

♠ 10 8 7 5
♡ A 2
◇ K 7 6 3
♣ 6 5 2

♠ A 2
♡ Q J 9 7 5 3
◇ 8
♣ Q 10 8 7

♠ K J 3
♡ 10 8 6
◇ J 9 5 2
♣ J 9 3

♠ Q 9 6 4
♡ K 4
◇ A Q 10 4
♣ A K 4

West	North	East	South
Henry	**Sol**	**Ronnie**	**Jerry**
Bendig	**Steiner**	**Neuman**	**Blum**
-	-	-	1◇
1♡	2◇	Pass	2♠
Pass	3♠	Pass	4♠
All Pass			

Bendig led his singleton diamond and Sol Steiner laid out the dummy. 'At duplicate I would start with a negative double,' he observed.

'Why would anyone want to play duplicate?' asked Neuman. 'A game for old women and students, if you ask me. Nothing can beat high-stake rubber bridge.'

It depends on whether you win or lose, thought Blum. He would rather have five hundred dollars in his wallet than five hundred black points, it was true. Now, what were his chances here? The opening lead was surely a singleton. If he ran it to his hand, he would have to cross to ♡A to play on the trump suit. Even if a finesse of the nine drew an honour from West, there would be no entry to dummy to play on trumps again.

Blum leaned forward and played the king of diamonds to the first trick. A trump to the nine drew the West's ace and Blum won the queen of hearts switch with dummy's ace. When he led a second round of trumps East rose with the king and exited with the jack of trumps. Blum checked the lie of the diamond suit by cashing the ace and then crossed to the ten of trumps to take a marked finesse of the ten of diamonds. The game was his, for the loss of just two trumps and a club.

'A nice easy one, as it turned out,' Steiner observed. 'I know players who would have passed Two Spades on my cards!'

Blum smiled. It was an easy enough hand for someone who knew how to play the cards. The other three would surely have played low from dummy at Trick 1, not giving the matter any thought. There would have been no way to recover.

Blum pocketed a healthy $1700 at the end of the first chukker and then cut to partner Ronnie Neuman. A small man, bald-headed with silver spectacles, he had made his money from the car rental business. His wife had died the previous year, leaving their only son as the sole heir to the family fortune. Not rating him a worthy recipient of so much money, Neuman was doing his best to spend most of it before he died himself.

'Cappelletti against their notrump, Jerry?' queried Neuman.

'Fine,' Blum replied. 'It won't come up, of course, now you've mentioned it.'

After a failing part-score on the first deal, Bendig arrived in a slam.

North-South Game	♠ A 2		
Dealer North	♡ A Q 9 7		
	◇ 10 6 4 3		
	♣ Q 4 2		

♠ J 10 9 6 4		♠ Q 8 5 3
♡ 8 2	N W E S	♡ 5
◇ Q 7 2		◇ A 8 5
♣ J 8 5		♣ 10 9 7 6 3

♠ K 7
♡ K J 10 6 4 3
◇ K J 9
♣ A K

West	North	East	South
Jerry	**Sol**	**Ronnie**	**Henry**
Blum	**Steiner**	**Neuman**	**Bendig**
-	1◇	Pass	1♡
Pass	2♡	Pass	4NT
Pass	5♡	Pass	6♡
All Pass			

Blum led the jack of spades, won in the dummy. After drawing trumps with the ace and king, Bendig played the two top clubs in his hand. He then crossed to dummy with a third round of trumps and cashed the queen of clubs, throwing an ostentatious jack of diamonds. The key moment had arrived. Declarer now led a low diamond from dummy.

Ronnie Neuman had seen declarer's ◇J and lost no time in rising with the ace. Bendig triumphantly faced his hand. 'I have the rest,' he said.

Blum gritted his teeth. Jeez! The contract had been on a diamond guess and Ronnie had gone up with the ace.

Neuman looked apologetically towards Blum. 'Didn't think he had two diamonds left,' he said. 'Knowin' Henry, he'd get it right anyway.'

Blum managed a weak smile. Of course declarer wouldn't have got it right! If a player like Ronnie didn't produce the ace in that situation it was a near certainty that he didn't hold it. Apart from that, suppose his ace of diamonds had picked up the bare king from declarer. Where is Heaven's name did Ronnie think a second trick was coming from? Declarer surely held the spade king, so he could have no further loser.

Blum scribbled the horrible result on his scorepad. His partner's ace of diamonds play had cost him one and a half grand.

Blum's mood was not improved when he picked up a feeble two-count on the next deal. Prospects improved when his partner opened the bidding but the opponents were soon in game. This was the deal:

East-West Game
Dealer East

♠ K Q 7 4
♡ K 10 4
◇ A J 3
♣ Q 6 4

♠ 9 5 3
♡ Q 7
◇ 6 5 4 2
♣ 9 8 7 3

```
  N
W   E
  S
```

♠ 2
♡ J 8 3 2
◇ K Q 8 7
♣ A K J 10

♠ A J 10 8 6
♡ A 9 6 5
◇ 10 9
♣ 5 2

West	North	East	South
Jerry	**Sol**	**Ronnie**	**Henry**
Blum	**Steiner**	**Neuman**	**Bendig**
-	-	1♣	1♠
Pass	4♠	All Pass	

Blum led the nine of clubs against Four Spades and Neuman played three rounds of the suit, declarer ruffing the third round. After drawing trumps in three rounds, declarer ran the ten of diamonds to East's queen. Neuman had to find an exit in this end position:

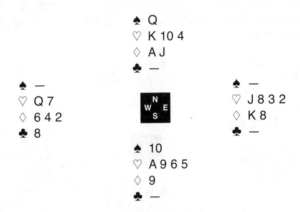

Even with a gun pointed at his head, Neuman would not return a diamond into dummy's tenace. He spun the heart two on to the table and Blum's queen forced dummy's king. When the ten of hearts was covered by the jack and ace Bendig had the remaining tricks. The nine of hearts was good and he could ruff the fourth round of hearts in dummy.

'Clever end-play, Henry,' said Neuman. He nodded happily, almost as if he were pleased that his son would now be deprived of a further big sum.

Blum was less pleased. What was this heart return from Ronnie? A diamond return would have given declarer no chance. He could throw one heart away but there would still be an unavoidable loser in the suit.

'You should return a diamond, Ronnie,' said Henry Bendig.

'With the ace-jack in the dummy?' Neuman exclaimed. 'Are you mad? I was hoping to make a diamond at the end.'

'If I had ace-queen-one in hearts and three diamonds, I'd have cashed the hearts first,' Bendig continued. 'You'd have been endplayed when you won the first diamond.'

'How do I know what you've got?' Neuman protested. 'You might have two hearts and four diamonds, for all I can tell.'

'With ace-one of hearts I would take just two rounds of trumps,' said Bendig. 'Then I'd ruff out the hearts and end-play you in diamonds.'

This was too much for Neuman to follow. 'You may be right, as the cards lie,' he replied gruffly. 'That doesn't mean I'm ever going to lead into a diamond tenace that's before my eyes. That's a plain stupid thing to do.'

The second chukker drew to a close with a part-score deal and Blum had to hand over more than two thousand dollars, wiping out his earlier profit. His next partner would be Henry Bendig, who was a better player than the other two. Sol Steiner made an easy 3NT against them on the first deal of the next chukker. This was the second deal:

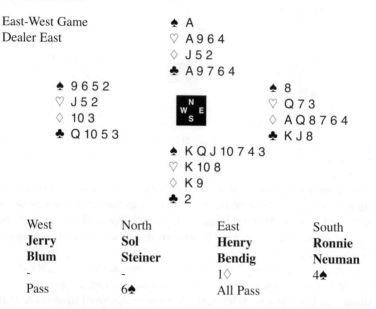

West	North	East	South
Jerry	**Sol**	**Henry**	**Ronnie**
Blum	**Steiner**	**Bendig**	**Neuman**
-	-	1◇	4♠
Pass	6♠	All Pass	

Blum was not pleased to find that yet again a grand was riding on a single deal. What had he done to deserve this? He led the ten of diamonds, his partner winning with the ace and returning a second diamond to declarer's king.

Ronnie Neuman was not overjoyed at his prospects. Sol might hold three aces but there was nothing much else in his hand. What was he meant to do with the potential loser in hearts? Eat it? He could set up the clubs if the suit broke 4-3 but there would be no entry to reach the long card in the suit. Ah well, there was nothing else to try.

A club to the ace was followed by a club ruff, a trump to the ace, and a second club ruff. Neuman now ran all his trumps. Jerry would doubtless hold on to the right cards but with Henry setting East, well, there was always a chance he would do the wrong thing. This end position was soon reached:

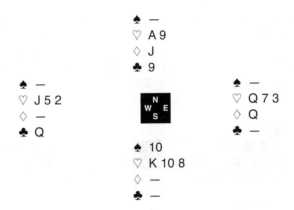

♠ —
♡ A 9
◇ J
♣ 9

♠ —
♡ J 5 2
◇ —
♣ Q

♠ —
♡ Q 7 3
◇ Q
♣ —

♠ 10
♡ K 10 8
◇ —
♣ —

When the last spade was led Blum had to throw a heart in order to keep a guard against dummy's ♣9. The club was thrown from dummy and Bendig, sitting East, found himself in a similar predicament. To prevent dummy's ◇J from scoring a trick he had to keep the queen of that suit and release a heart.

Neuman now played three rounds of hearts, delighted to see the queen and jack fall on the second round. The third round of hearts was his and the slam had been made. 'When in doubt run the long suit!' Neuman exclaimed. 'How many contracts have I made by doing that? Even against good players it can work.'

'There was nothing we could do, Ronnie,' said Blum. 'We were squeezed, both of us. You played it well.'

'Just the right moment for such a hand!' Neuman exclaimed. 'Only a good player like Jerry can appreciate a squeeze like that.'

Blum was looking somewhat pale. Appreciate it? Appreciate a deal that had wiped out his entire earnings of the previous week? He looked across at his partner. 'We can beat it, you know,' he said. 'Ronnie needed to ruff two clubs to leave me guarding the suit. If you return a trump at Trick 2, you remove an entry to the dummy. He can't manage it.'

'And you would like me to do that if you have a singleton diamond?' said Bendig. He laughed to himself. 'I can just see your face.'

'The diamond nine fell from declarer,' Blum persisted. 'You could place me with ten doubleton after that.'

Bendig tapped the side of his nose. 'You think Ronnie isn't clever enough to drop the nine from king-nine third?' he replied. 'The day I don't return a diamond on such a hand is the day I will give up the game.'

'Of course I drop the nine from king-nine-one,' Neuman declared. 'I wasn't born yesterday, or the day before.'

Bendig went one down in a part score on the next deal. This was the last deal of the chukker:

```
Game All              ♠ J 10 9 2
Dealer West           ♡ 3 2
                      ◇ K Q J 9 5
                      ♣ 6 4
  ♠ 5                              ♠ K 8 7 4
  ♡ A 10 8 4          N            ♡ Q J 9 7 5
  ◇ 10 8 6          W   E          ◇ 4 3 2
  ♣ J 10 9 7 5        S            ♣ 3
                      ♠ A Q 6 3
                      ♡ K 6
                      ◇ A 7
                      ♣ A K Q 8 2
```

West	North	East	South
Jerry	**Sol**	**Henry**	**Ronnie**
Blum	**Steiner**	**Bendig**	**Neuman**
Pass	Pass	Pass	1♣
Pass	1◇	Pass	2♠
Pass	4♠	Pass	6♠
All Pass			

Blum pinched the flesh of his thumb to make sure that this was not some horrible dream. The opponents were in a slam again? This was one of those days when he should have stayed in bed.

What to lead? The other three would have reached immediately for the ace of hearts, not giving the matter any thought. It was not his style to lead aces against a slam. It might be right on this particular deal, if partner held a trump trick, but an ace lead was much more likely to assist declarer.

Blum led the jack of clubs and down went the dummy. 'Not so much there, Sol,' observed Neuman. 'When you jumped to game I was expecting much more. I nearly bid a grand.'

Steiner lit up yet another cigarette. 'Four Spades is a weak bid,' he replied. 'We were forced to game already, so Four Spades is weaker than Three Spades.'

'Ah, don't give me that duplicate rubbish!' Neuman exclaimed. 'At Chicago, Four Spades is strong, believe me.'

Declarer won the club lead with the ace and crossed to dummy by playing the ace and king of diamonds. Muttering some prayer under his breath, he then ran the jack of trumps. His God was with him and the jack won the trick. When he continued with the ten of trumps East played low again. The ten was run and West showed out, discarding a heart. Neuman adjusted his silver-rimmed spectacles. What now?

He soon saw how the hand should be played. He led another top diamond from dummy and threw a heart when East followed suit. When he played another diamond winner, East ruffed and he overruffed. After drawing East's last trump with the ace, Neuman played two more top clubs and ruffed a club in dummy. Dummy's last diamond brought him his twelfth trick and the small slam had been made.

'Such a play I made there,' Neuman exclaimed. 'You were watching, Sol? All the suits break terribly but I still come home!'

Steiner blew out a large cloud of smoke. 'You should try playing duplicate, Ronnie,' he said. 'You would do well.'

The difference on the third chukker was more than three and a half grand. Bendig would not raise an eyebrow if his wife spent so much in an afternoon's shopping but it was serious money for Blum. He counted out a sheaf of hundred-dollar bills and looked down at his empty glass. 'You got any more of this bourbon, Sol?' he asked.

Play continued for another rotation of partners but the hands were relatively dull. Blum dropped a few hundred more and was soon in his blue Taurus, heading back through light traffic towards West Palm Beach.

The afternoon had cost him over four grand! Blum thought back to a similarly disastrous session, many years ago, that had brought his first marriage to an end. Annie had always been happy enough to accept the spoils of a winning session. When he had come back that evening and told her of the heavy loss, there had been a fearful row – one of many during the four and a half years they were together. He should have learnt his lesson after his tempestuous time with Lucille, but then there had been Jeanette. Seven years that marriage had lasted, the longest of the three.

Did he regret marrying any of them? It was difficult to say. Not that he would ever take the plunge again, thought Blum as he turned his car off the highway. No, he would pick up a six-pack of Coors, switch on the TV and watch the ball game tonight. With Dempster pitching, the Marlins must be in with a chance. There would be no-one to tell him he had drunk four bottles already and no-one wanting to switch over to some silly film on another channel.

Blum forced a smile to his lips. Being single did have some advantages.

9
A Date with Betsy

Blum always enjoyed playing at the spacious Tamarac Club in Fort Lauderdale. The atmosphere was friendly and the air conditioning was little short of heavenly. As for the bridge itself, there was never any pressure on him. Betsy didn't mind winning once in a  while, sure, but if they finished in the middle of the field she still enjoyed herself. A widow for over twenty years, she was happy to be seen with a good-looking professional across the table.

'You look younger every time I see you!' exclaimed Blum, as he met Betsy in the coffee room.

'It's true,' said Betsy, laughing. 'I scarcely look a day over seventy-five.'

'Have you drawn a position for us?' asked Blum.

'I should have let you do it for us,' Betsy replied. 'We are East-West and now I will have to move around.'

'You should ask them for a North-South position,' said Blum. 'I'm sure they'd be happy to do that.'

'I haven't reached that stage, thank goodness!' Betsy exclaimed. 'Why, I'm not even eighty until November.'

Blum made a mental note of this. He would have to find the exact date and send her some flowers and a card. Such little touches meant a lot to a client – sometimes even more than finishing in the black points.

On the first round Jerry and Betsy took their seats against the red-faced Jim Becker, a notorious overbidder. Although he was seriously overweight and had some difficulty in walking, he always wore a ranch shirt and cowboy boots. In his own mind he was doubtless a fine figure of a man.

'How're you doin', Betsy?' asked Becker.

'All the better for seeing you,' Betsy replied. She leaned forward and lowered her voice to a whisper. 'Did you try that diet I suggested?'

'I ain't tried it yet, Betsy, but I sure thought about tryin' it,' Becker replied. 'Don't much like prunes, that's the problem.'

'You're not meant to enjoy it,' Betsy reprimanded. 'They probably put prunes in the diet deliberately because no-one would want to eat too many.'

Becker made a straightforward 3NT on the first board of the round. This was the second board:

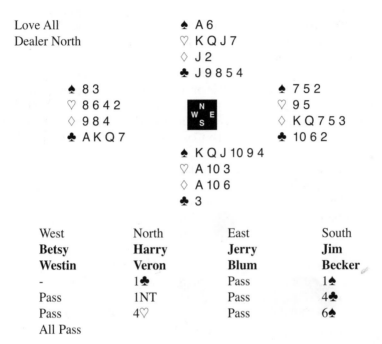

Love All	♠ A 6		
Dealer North	♡ K Q J 7		
	◇ J 2		
	♣ J 9 8 5 4		

West	North	East	South
Betsy	**Harry**	**Jerry**	**Jim**
Westin	**Veron**	**Blum**	**Becker**
-	1♣	Pass	1♠
Pass	1NT	Pass	4♣
Pass	4♡	Pass	6♠
All Pass			

Becker promoted himself to a small slam, via Gerber, and Betsy led ♣K, drawing the four, two and three. What next? Declarer surely held the two red aces, so a switch in that direction was no good. It was unlikely that declarer held a second club but... that seemed to be the only chance.

When a second high club appeared on the table, Becker ruffed in his hand. The king and ace of trumps were followed by a second club ruff, both defenders following. Declarer crossed to the king of hearts and took a third club ruff in his hand, establishing a long card in the suit. Ace of hearts and a heart to the queen put him back in dummy. He then discarded his two diamond losers, one on the established club and another on the fourth round of hearts.

'Only twenty-six points between us!' Becker announced proudly. 'That should be a top.'

'Nothing I could do,' said Betsy. 'I knew he had both the red aces.'

Blum made no comment. Some of his clients were keen to improve their game and welcomed any instruction from the pro. Facing one of them, he would have pointed out how the hand should be defended. King of clubs lead, to request a count signal, and then switch to another suit when partner's ♣2 showed that declarer had a singleton. Declarer would not then have had enough entries to set up and enjoy a long club.

Betsy rose to her feet as the change of round was called. 'Don't forget about the prunes, Jim,' she said. 'You'll soon get used to them.'

A round or two later, Blum and Betsy faced two of the club regulars, Gayle Loope and Mary Parker. It was well known that they did not approve of members bringing professional partners into the club. Was it right that Betsy should finish ahead of them, just because she could afford to sign a big cheque at the end? They looked sniffily at Betsy as she took her seat. She should be ashamed of herself!

This was the first board of the round:

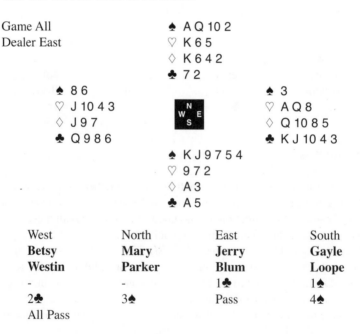

```
Game All          ♠ A Q 10 2
Dealer East       ♡ K 6 5
                  ◇ K 6 4 2
                  ♣ 7 2
    ♠ 8 6                         ♠ 3
    ♡ J 10 4 3         N          ♡ A Q 8
    ◇ J 9 7         W     E       ◇ Q 10 8 5
    ♣ Q 9 8 6          S          ♣ K J 10 4 3
                  ♠ K J 9 7 5 4
                  ♡ 9 7 2
                  ◇ A 3
                  ♣ A 5
```

West	North	East	South
Betsy	**Mary**	**Jerry**	**Gayle**
Westin	**Parker**	**Blum**	**Loope**
-	-	1♣	1♠
2♣	3♠	Pass	4♠
All Pass			

The opponents arrived in Four Spades and Betsy led ♣6. 'Play small,' said the elegantly coiffed declarer.

After only a moment's pause Blum contributed the three to the trick. Declarer won with the ace and drew trumps in two rounds. Hoping that something good would happen, she then exited with a club. Blum allowed Betsy's eight of clubs to win the trick and was pleased to see the jack of hearts appear on the table next. Gayle Loope did not like the look of this card at all. 'Play small,' she said.

The jack won the trick and Betsy continued with a low heart. The declarer paused to consider the lie of the heart suit. Jerry had opened the bidding and almost certainly held the ace of hearts. Could it be doubleton?

'It doesn't matter what you do,' said Blum softly.

Gayle Loope gave an annoyed shake of the head. 'Play the king, then,' she said. Blum scored two more heart tricks and the game was one down.

'Nice heart switch, partner,' said Blum.

'Thank you,' said Betsy, hoping that the compliment had been heard on the adjacent tables. 'You were showing off a bit at Trick 1, weren't you? Playing your three!'

'No, no, it was necessary,' Blum replied. 'If I play an honour, Gayle will let it win. She wins the next club, draws trumps, plays two diamonds and ruffs a diamond. Then she goes back to dummy with a trump and throws me in with the fourth round of diamonds, discarding a heart. I'm endplayed.'

Gayle Loope had not followed a word of this. Indeed, she looked somewhat dazed by trying to follow it. 'That's exactly how I would have played it,' she said. 'Your partner would be endplayed, Betsy.'

'Of course if Gayle lets your six of clubs hold, you would switch straight away to the jack of hearts,' continued Blum.

Betsy nodded enthusiastically. 'I certainly would,' she declared.

It occurred to Blum that his partner had led the only card of her thirteen that would allow the game to be made. If declarer had only covered the six of clubs with dummy's seven, she could have forced him to win the trick and made the contract! Suppose West had led the $\diamond$7 instead. Against a skilled declarer Blum would need to play the five. If he contributed any higher card, declarer could duck and subsequently discard a club on the third round of diamonds. After eliminating the club suit, it would again be possible to endplay East on the fourth round of diamonds.

This was the second board of the round:

Love All ♠ 10 2
Dealer South ♡ A Q 9 7 6
 ◇ K 7 6
 ♣ Q 8 4

♠ 9 8 7 5 4		♠ A J 6 3
♡ 5 4 2	N W E S	♡ 3
◇ 8 4		◇ Q J 10 5 2
♣ J 9 2		♣ A 6 5

 ♠ K Q
 ♡ K J 10 8
 ◇ A 9 3
 ♣ K 10 7 3

West	North	East	South
Betsy	**Mary**	**Jerry**	**Gayle**
Westin	**Parker**	**Blum**	**Loope**
-	-	-	1NT
Pass	2◇	Pass	2♡
Pass	3NT	Pass	4♡
All Pass			

Against the heart game Betsy led the eight of spades, her second-best card to indicate a poor holding in the suit. Blum won with the ace and switched to the queen of diamonds, which ran to dummy's king. Declarer drew trumps in three rounds and then decided to play on clubs, hoping to set up a discard for her losing diamond.

When a club was played to the queen, Blum had an almost complete picture of the deal. Betsy had played the eight on the first round of diamonds, a high card that indicated a doubleton in the suit. On the first round of clubs she had played the two, a low card to show an odd number of clubs. If he won the first round of clubs with the ace and cleared the diamond suit, Betsy would have no diamond to play when she won the second or third round of clubs. Declarer would then be able to discard dummy's last diamond on the long club in the South hand.

With a smoothness that impressed even himself, Blum allowed the queen of clubs to win. Gayle Loope continued with a club to the ten, losing to West's jack. Betsy was quick to clear the defenders' diamond trick and when Blum won the third round of clubs he cashed a diamond to put the game one down.

Gayle Loope looked resentfully in Blum's direction. 'Did you duck that ace of clubs on purpose?' she demanded. 'It was a very risky play. I could have made one trick with the queen and another with the king.'

'It was a risk I had to take,' Blum replied. 'Since Betsy held only two diamonds, I needed her to take our first trick in clubs.'

Betsy surprised all present on the next few rounds, playing several hands rather well. They then reached the table where Big Al occupied the South seat. A former owner of the club, he was now the resident professional. 'How's business, Jerry?' he growled. 'I see you still manage to pick up the best-lookin' clients.'

Betsy patted Big Al appreciatively on the hand. 'Such a smooth talker,' she said. 'You don't do so badly yourself. Henrietta looks very smart today.'

Realising his gaffe, Big Al delivered a wide smile in the direction of his own, rather overdressed, partner. 'She sure does and she's been playin' real nice too.'

The players drew their cards for this board:

```
Game All              ♠ K 7
Dealer East           ♡ A 10 8
                      ◇ J 10 7
                      ♣ 9 7 6 3 2
        ♠ Q 10 6 3                      ♠ 8 4
        ♡ K Q 9 5 4        N           ♡ J 7 6 3 2
        ◇ A 2           W     E         ◇ 8 3
        ♣ Q 4             S             ♣ K J 10 5
                      ♠ A J 9 5 2
                      ♡ —
                      ◇ K Q 9 6 5 4
                      ♣ A 8
```

West	North	East	South
Betsy	**Henrietta**	**Jerry**	**Big**
Westin	**Tabbush**	**Blum**	**Al**
-	-	-	1♠
2♡	2♠	Pass	4♠
All Pass			

With little chance of winning the auction, Blum declined to support his partner's hearts. Betsy led the king of hearts against the resultant game in spades and down went the dummy. 'Only two spades for you,' said Henrietta apologetically, 'but I didn't like to pass with eight points.'

'Nice bid,' said Big Al.

He won the heart opening lead with dummy's ace and discarded a club from his hand. His next move would not have occurred to many players at the club – he cashed the king and ace of trumps. Leaving two trumps at large, he then cleared the diamond suit. Ten tricks were soon in the bag and it only remained for Henrietta to fill out the scoresheet. 'It's a nice top for us!' she declared. 'Only two other pairs bid Four Spades and they both went down.'

'Do you see why I didn't take a trump finesse?' asked Big Al.

'Of course,' Henrietta replied brightly. 'You didn't want to risk a diamond ruff.'

'It wasn't that,' continued Big Al. 'If a finesse loses and they take a diamond ruff, I still make ten tricks.'

'It was because Betsy had overcalled,' said Henrietta. 'That's it. You knew that the finesse would lose!'

'No, no,' replied Big Al. 'Suppose I take a finesse and lose to the queen. Betsy will force me with a heart and I'll lose control of the hand unless trumps are 3-3. Since we were in a game that wouldn't be bid too often, it was right to play safely for ten tricks.'

Henrietta Tabbush surveyed the scene contentedly. What a pleasure it was to have a professional playing the dummy for her. Almost as satisfying as a body massage at her local health club. It cost more than a massage, it was true, but… well, Stanley had left her a large fortune and she couldn't take it with her. Nothing was cheap nowadays, anyway.

Blum was hoping to play the next hand himself, to retrieve a few matchpoints. No, it was once again Big Al who ended as declarer.

East-West Game	♠ Q J 4 3	
Dealer East	♡ —	
	◇ K 10 9 8 6 4	
	♣ J 6 2	

	♠ 6 2		♠ 7
	♡ A K Q 9 6	N / W E / S	♡ J 10 5
	◇ Q 7 3		◇ A J 5 2
	♣ Q 10 8		♣ K 9 7 5 3

	♠ A K 10 9 8 5	
	♡ 8 7 4 3 2	
	◇ —	
	♣ A 4	

West	North	East	South
Betsy	**Henrietta**	**Jerry**	**Big**
Westin	**Tabbush**	**Blum**	**Al**
-	-	-	1♠
2♡	4♡	Pass	6♠
All Pass			

Without asking what North's 4♡ bid had meant, Betsy led the ace of hearts. 'Nice dummy,' said Big Al, in a tone that could not be deciphered. 'Ruff it.'

When declarer called for the ten of diamonds, Blum played low without giving anything away. Big Al threw a club and West's diamond queen won the trick. The trump switch was won by dummy's queen and declarer then had a key decision to take. Should he simply ruff two diamonds, hoping to drop an original A-Q-x with West? Or should he take a double ruffing finesse through East, playing for him to hold the ace and the jack.

Other things being equal, it would doubtless have been better odds after West's overcall to try to ruff down the ace. Big Al knew his customers, however. There was no way that Betsy would not have asked a few searching questions about the bidding if she held two aces. Such players hated to miss a double when there were two aces to cash. 'Play the king of diamonds,' said Big Al.

Blum withheld the ace but declarer was committed to his line. He discarded a heart and West followed powerlessly with a low diamond. The nine of diamonds was covered by the ace and ruffed. A second round of trumps to the jack allowed declarer to take a further diamond ruff. The long diamonds could be reached with a heart ruff and the slam had been made.

'Seven Hearts is only two down, Jerry!' Betsy exclaimed. 'Did you think of sacrificing? I did bid hearts.'

An amused Blum shook his head. Just three-card trump support, with an ace and a king to aid the defence? No, it had not occurred to him to sacrifice at the seven-level, vulnerable against not. If declarer hadn't read the cards so well he would have gone down, anyway.

'Seven Hearts can go three down on a diamond lead,' observed Big Al. 'I ruff and underlead in spades to get a second ruff.'

'It's still cheaper than you making Six Spades,' Betsy persisted. 'If Jerry bids Five Hearts over Henrietta's Four Hearts, I'd sacrifice on my hand. I have hardly any defence outside the heart suit.'

The two pros gave up the fight. Clients were notorious result merchants and always had been. If a vulnerable seven-level sacrifice would have paid off, in their eyes it should have been bid.

As the rounds ticked by, Blum took advantage of several opportunities to improve the partnership's score. He put them at around 58% as the last round started. Their opponents were Harry Kirkbride and his wife, Penny. Kirkbride fancied himself as a dummy player and rarely allowed his wife to play a hand. This was the first board of the round:

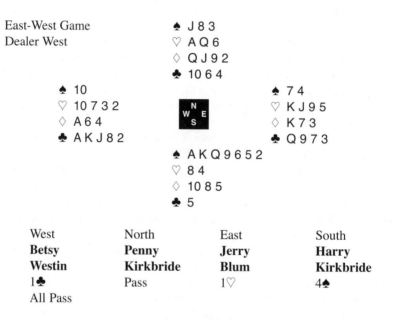

East-West Game
Dealer West

♠ J 8 3
♡ A Q 6
◊ Q J 9 2
♣ 10 6 4

♠ 10
♡ 10 7 3 2
◊ A 6 4
♣ A K J 8 2

♠ 7 4
♡ K J 9 5
◊ K 7 3
♣ Q 9 7 3

♠ A K Q 9 6 5 2
♡ 8 4
◊ 10 8 5
♣ 5

West	North	East	South
Betsy	**Penny**	**Jerry**	**Harry**
Westin	**Kirkbride**	**Blum**	**Kirkbride**
1♣	Pass	1♡	4♠
All Pass			

Betsy thought for a while over the 4♠ intervention, eventually deciding to pass. Blum did not have enough to compete with 5♣ and would have been reluctant to bid anyway, after his partner's hesitation. He passed out the spade game and Betsy led the king of clubs.

Blum had taught Betsy the idea of playing count signals on a king lead and he therefore contributed the nine to the trick. He stole a brief glance across the table. Had she registered the card? Surely it should be obvious to her that he held four clubs rather than two, with South being so long in spades. It might then occur to her to switch to hearts, setting up a trick or two before declarer could get the diamonds going.

At Trick 2 Betsy continued with the ace of clubs. Kirkbride ruffed and drew trumps with the ace and king. He then led a low diamond towards the dummy. Once more Blum looked briefly across the table. Rise with the ace and switch to a heart, partner!

Betsy followed with a low diamond and the queen was played from dummy. Blum could see that it was the end of the road if he won the trick. He could not attack hearts from his side of the table and declarer would be able to ruff a club return and set up the diamond suit. Blum allowed dummy's queen of diamonds to win and Kirkbride returned to his hand with a club ruff. When a second round of diamonds was led from the South hand, Blum closed his eyes for a moment. This is your last chance, partner. The ace of diamonds, please!

Blum opened his eyes to see Betsy's ace of diamonds on the table. She switched to a heart and the game was one down.

'Good thing I was awake there,' observed Betsy. 'If I don't rush up with the ace and switch to a heart, he makes it!'

Blum nodded enthusiastically. 'Yes, indeed,' he replied. 'You defended very well.'

Betsy smiled happily as she returned her cards to the wallet. Defence had been the weakest part of her game before she met Jerry. Now – thanks to his help – she could defend with the best of them!

10
Swiss in Miami

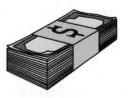

Blum had three regular clients in Miami, along with several others who occasionally called him up. On his present visit he was to play in a two-session sectional event, the White Pelican Swiss Teams. His partner would be one of the regulars, a long-retired banker called Walter Kreisler. Their team mates were two of Kreisler's banking friends, no experts but strong enough players to achieve a respectable finish.

'We start on Table 56, Jerry,' said Kreisler. 'You're feeling lucky today?'

'I always feel lucky, playing with you,' Blum replied. 'We might be even luckier than usual if you'd let me play a hand or two!'

Kreisler laughed. 'You know how I hate being dummy, Jerry,' he replied. 'When you hold the spades, then I will let you play the contract!'

The first round started and the opponents at Blum's table turned out to be elderly and relatively inexperienced. This was an early board:

East-West Game Dealer South	♠ 10 9 3 2 ♡ 9 7 5 4 ◇ 9 6 5 ♣ J 5	
♠ 8 6 5 ♡ Q 8 ◇ 8 7 2 ♣ K Q 9 7 4		♠ 4 ♡ J 10 3 2 ◇ A J 10 4 ♣ 10 6 3 2
	♠ A K Q J 7 ♡ A K 6 ◇ K Q 3 ♣ A 8	

West	North	East	South
Richard	**Walter**	**Josie**	**Jerry**
Caldino	**Kreisler**	**Caldino**	**Blum**
-	-	-	2♣
Pass	2♦	Pass	2♠
Pass	2NT	Pass	3NT
Pass	4♠	All Pass	

The king of clubs was led and down went the dummy. 'You see?' Kreisler exclaimed. 'Did I pass 3NT? No, when you have the spades you can play the contract.'

The opponents looked up uncertainly.

'Just a private joke,' Blum explained. 'I'm only allowed to play one hand in ten and my moment has arrived.'

Blum won the club lead with the ace and drew trumps in three rounds, leaving the trump ten as an entry to the dummy. When he played his two top hearts the queen fell from West. Blum saw that there was no need to play a third round of hearts himself, risking a damaging force on the fourth round if West's queen was indeed a doubleton. Instead, he exited in clubs. If West held another heart and chose to play it at this stage, the suit would break 3-3 and he could throw a diamond on dummy's long card in the suit.

West won the second round of clubs and exited with the eight of diamonds, covered by dummy's nine. Realising that declarer must hold the king and queen of the suit, Josie Caldino contributed the ten to the trick. Blum won with the king and these cards remained:

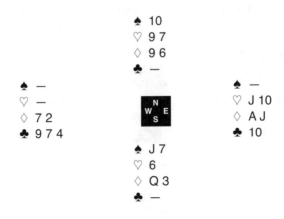

```
                    ♠ 10
                    ♡ 9 7
                    ◇ 9 6
                    ♣ —
  ♠ —                             ♠ —
  ♡ —                             ♡ J 10
  ◇ 7 2          N                ◇ A J
  ♣ 9 7 4      W   E              ♣ 10
                    S
                    ♠ J 7
                    ♡ 6
                    ◇ Q 3
                    ♣ —
```

Blum now had to read how the cards lay. The appearance of West's queen of hearts suggested, according to the Principle of Restricted Choice, that he had no further heart in his hand. If so, it would cost the contract to play on hearts now. In any case, West's switch to the eight of diamonds strongly suggested that the ace of diamonds lay with East. His mind made up, Blum played the seven of trumps to dummy's ten. He then led a second round of diamonds towards the queen. East did indeed hold the diamond ace and ten tricks were his.

'That was a struggle,' Kreisler observed. 'Perhaps I should have left it in 3NT.'

'It depends what this lady leads,' Blum replied. 'There would be no hope at all on a club lead.'

'I was ready to lead a club,' said Josie Caldino.

On the next board, vulnerable against not, Blum picked up this hand:

♠ A K 6 5 3
♡ A
◇ 10 9 5 2
♣ Q 10 5

He opened 1♠ and West overcalled 2♣. Kreisler then jumped to 4♣, a splinter bid showing a sound game-raise in spades with at most one club. With very little pause East contested with 5♣.

Blum surveyed his hand once more. Only a 13-count, yes, but he would need next to nothing from partner to make a slam. The fact that the opponents had contested the auction to the five-level strongly suggested that Kreisler was void in clubs. In that case as little as the king-queen of diamonds and the queen of spades might be enough to yield twelve tricks. Blum jumped to 6♠ and there was no further bidding. The king of clubs was led and this proved to be the whole deal:

North-South Game
Dealer East

	♠ 10 8 7 4 2	
	♡ K J 8 7 5	
	◇ Q 6 4	
	♣ —	
♠ Q		♠ J 9
♡ 10 6 4 3		♡ Q 9 2
◇ K 3		◇ A J 8 7
♣ A K 9 7 6 3		♣ J 8 4 2
	♠ A K 6 5 3	
	♡ A	
	◇ 10 9 5 2	
	♣ Q 10 5	

West	North	East	South
Richard	**Walter**	**Josie**	**Jerry**
Caldino	**Kreisler**	**Caldino**	**Blum**
-	-	Pass	1♠
2♣	4♣	5♣	6♠
All Pass			

Blum raised an eyebrow at the threadbare dummy. Only six points? Even just the king of diamonds instead of the queen would have given the slam some kind of play.

Blum ruffed the club lead in dummy, drew trumps in two rounds and cashed the ace of hearts. A club ruff returned the lead to the table and he cashed the king of hearts, throwing a diamond. 'Small heart, please,' he said.

By good fortune, the queen of hearts fell on this trick. Blum was then able to ruff his last club and discard two more diamond losers on the jack and eight of hearts.

'You made it?' queried Kreisler.

'Yes, it was a bit lucky,' Blum replied.

Josie Caldino looked sternly at her husband. 'You didn't have the diamond king, did you?' she enquired in a New York accent.

'I did,' he replied.

'I had the ace!' Josie exclaimed. 'We can cash the ace and king, unless...' she turned towards Blum. 'Did you have a singleton diamond?'

'No, no, I had four,' Blum replied.

Richard Caldino leaned across the table to inspect his wife's cards. 'We can score three diamond tricks,' he said. 'I lead the king and then you make the ace and the jack.'

'That would be two down,' Josie concluded. 'A nice top for us.'

'In fact, I think you can make another trick,' Kreisler informed the East player. 'If you continue with a fourth round of diamonds, that promotes a trump trick for you.'

Josie Caldino surveyed Kreisler disapprovingly. 'I can't think why you bid a slam when even the game is down off the top,' she told him. 'You only had about twenty points between you.'

Play proceeded and two or three boards later a competitive deal arose:

East-West Game
Dealer North

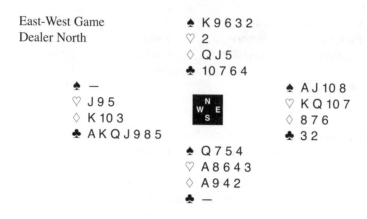

		♠ K 9 6 3 2
		♡ 2
		◇ Q J 5
		♣ 10 7 6 4

♠ —		♠ A J 10 8
♡ J 9 5		♡ K Q 10 7
◇ K 10 3		◇ 8 7 6
♣ A K Q J 9 8 5		♣ 3 2

	♠ Q 7 5 4	
	♡ A 8 6 4 3	
	◇ A 9 4 2	
	♣ —	

West	North	East	South
Ralph	**Walter**	**Josie**	**Jerry**
Caldino	**Kreisler**	**Caldino**	**Blum**
-	Pass	Pass	1♡
2♣	Dble	2NT	3♠
3NT	Pass	Pass	4♠
Pass	Pass	Dble	All Pass

Hoping that his partner's club holding would not have embarrassed declarer in 3NT, Blum decided to sacrifice in Four Spades. West thought for a while about bidding Five Clubs over this. Perhaps sensing some vibes from an Easterly direction, he eventually decided to pass and leave the decision to his wife. Josie Caldino was in doubt what to do. She slapped the red Double card onto the table and there was no further bidding. Despite his wife's admonitions on the earlier board, Ralph Caldino launched the defence with the king of clubs.

Blum ruffed the club lead, cashed the ace of hearts and ruffed a heart. Since he would need to take whatever diamond tricks he could before proceeding with the cross-ruff, he next ran the queen of diamonds. West won with the king and, with no trump to play, returned another high club.

Blum ruffed in his hand and took a second heart ruff in dummy. He then steeled himself to play two more rounds of diamonds before one or other defender could take a discard in the suit. Luck was with him when the two diamonds stood up. A third heart ruff left the lead in dummy with these cards still to be played:

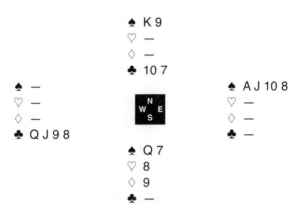

♠ K 9
♥ —
♦ —
♣ 10 7

♠ —   ♠ A J 10 8
♥ —   ♥ —
♦ —   ♦ —
♣ Q J 9 8   ♣ —

♠ Q 7
♥ 8
♦ 9
♣ —

Blum, who had so far lost only one trick, called for a club from dummy. When East ruffed with the eight, Blum overruffed with the queen and exited with a heart, discarding the last club. Josie Caldino could barely believe it when she had to ruff and concede the last trick to dummy's king of trumps. The doubled game had been made.

'I knew I should have bid Five Clubs,' Ralph Caldino declared. 'The void spade should have been a warning to me.'

'Five Clubs is murdered!' his wife exclaimed. 'Heart to the ace, heart ruff, diamond to the ace, heart ruff. There's no entry to dummy now, so you would have to lose another diamond too. That's 800.'

'You may be right,' Caldino replied. 'I still think it was the right thing to do.'

The Kreisler team had won their first match 19-1 and were promoted to Table 4. In a national they could now expect some stiff opposition. Since it was only a sectional – in Miami, what's more – it was no surprise to Blum when he took his seat against another elderly couple.

'You play Standard?' asked Joe Donner, whose white crew-cut hair contrasted starkly with his sun-tanned face.

'Yep,' Kreisler replied. 'Jerry Blum and I play one or two gadgets on the side.'

The couple showed no recognition of the pro's name, not that Blum had expected they would, and play commenced with this deal:

East-West Game   ♠ 7 5 4
Dealer South   ♡ J
                      ◊ 8 7 5 3 2
                      ♣ 10 6 4 3

	♠ K Q J 10 3		♠ 9 8 6 2
	♡ 8 7 6 4	N / W E / S	♡ A Q 5 3
	◊ A Q 10 4		◊ J 9 6
	♣ —		♣ J 9

                      ♠ A
                      ♡ K 10 9 2
                      ◊ K
                      ♣ A K Q 8 7 5 2

West	North	East	South
Joe	**Jerry**	**Alice**	**Walter**
Donner	**Blum**	**Donner**	**Kreisler**
-	-	-	1♣
1♠	Pass	2♠	3♡
4♠	5♣	All Pass	

Blum sacrificed on his one-count and was surprised when no double came. Ah well, perhaps Walter had his bid for a change.

West led the king of spades and Kreisler won with the ace. When he played the ace of trumps West showed out, discarding a spade. A heart to the jack lost to East's queen and she returned a second round of trumps. Kreisler now paused to consider the position. He had three losing hearts and only two trumps in dummy to deal with them. What to do?

Kreisler ruffed the nine of hearts, returned to his hand with a spade ruff and led the king of hearts. There was very little chance of ruffing out an original A-Q-x with East, so Kreisler eventually ran the heart king. East won with the ace and the game was one down.

'Nothing wrong with the bidding,' Kreisler declared. 'East held both the heart honours!'

Blum nodded sympathetically. It was not the moment to point out errors in his partner's play but it had been a poor idea to draw a round of trumps at Trick 2. If he had played on hearts immediately the entries would have been there to take three heart ruffs.

'They make Four Spades, so it's a good sacrifice,' Kreisler continued.

A good sacrifice, yes, thought Blum. Had he played the hand properly, it would have been a very good sacrifice.

Kreisler's other pair, George Havers and Jacob Simmonds, performed strongly in this match and another big win resulted, by a margin of 17-3.

Fifth position was the reward and Blum and his partner took their seats at Table 3 against two sixty-year-old men.

'You remember me?' asked Joe Speck as Blum took his seat.

Blum looked at the East player, trying to recall where he might have met him. 'You seem familiar,' he replied, 'but...'

'I played against you in Memphis,' Joe Speck continued. 'You must remember. I made an impossible 3NT and then Four Spades doubled.'

'I haven't played in Memphis this year,' Blum replied. 'You must be thinking of someone else.'

'I didn't say it was this year, did I?' Speck continued. 'No, it was maybe six or seven years ago. I never forget a hand or a face.'

Blum withdrew his cards from the wallet. If the guy had gone down in the two games, you could bet your bottom dollar he would have forgotten about it.

This was the first deal of the match:

```
North-South Game        ♠ Q J 10 7 5 3
Dealer East             ♡ Q 4
                        ◇ J 10 8
                        ♣ 10 9
      ♠ 8 6                              ♠ 9 4
      ♡ K 10 9 6 3         N             ♡ 8 7 2
      ◇ A 9 6 5 2       W     E          ◇ 7 4
      ♣ 5                  S             ♣ A Q J 8 7 4
                        ♠ A K 2
                        ♡ A J 5
                        ◇ K Q 3
                        ♣ K 6 3 2
```

West	North	East	South
Ralph	**Jerry**	**Joe**	**Walter**
Kohn	**Blum**	**Speck**	**Kreisler**
-	-	Pass	2NT
Pass	3♡	Pass	3♠
Pass	4♠	All Pass	

For a moment Blum was tempted to respond 4♠, to play the hand. When deciding between bids of roughly equal merit, he was happy to choose the one

115

that would leave him as declarer. Here, though, it could be important for the opening lead to run up to the strong hand. He responded with a transfer bid and then raised to game.

West led ♣5 and Joe Speck won with the ace. After a brief pause he returned ♣4. Kreisler put up the club king, preparing to draw trumps and take the heart finesse for an overtrick. That was his intention but West gave him a nasty surprise by ruffing the king of clubs. Declarer could not thereafter avoid two losers in the red suits and the game went one down.

'You gave him a chance to make it, Joe!' complained the West player. 'You should lead the queen of clubs at Trick 2, not a low one. If he runs the four to the ten, I'm ruffing a loser.'

Joe Speck smiled, shaking his head at the same time. 'So much you know about this game, Ralph,' he said. 'If I play back the queen of clubs, he can guess you have made a short-suit lead. Maybe it will occur to him not to cover.'

'Yes, yes, I see,' Kohn replied. 'He can ruff the third round of clubs in dummy and discard a heart on the king later. Yes, the low club return was a clever move.'

When scores were compared it turned out that the contract had been made at the other table.

'You led your singleton club?' asked Blum.

'Of course, but it made no difference,' replied Jacob Simmonds. 'She ducked the club return.'

'Good play to find,' observed Blum.

'Not so difficult,' said George Havers. 'After my 3♣ opening she knows the king will be ruffed.'

'Ah, you opened 3♣!' exclaimed Kreisler. 'Even I would get it right after that.'

A disappointing 10-10 draw in their third match relegated the Kreisler team to eleventh place at the half-time interval.

'We can still win it,' said Kreisler, wincing as he took a mouthful of the hotel coffee. 'This is meant to be coffee?' he exclaimed. 'A dollar fifty a cup and I expect something drinkable.'

'It's better than the stuff my wife makes,' George Havers observed. 'She drives ten miles to buy coffee at a place where it is cheap. Saves on her housekeeping money, but then I have to buy more gas for the car.'

Jacob Simmonds nodded sympathetically. 'Life was not meant to be easy,' he said.

Play restarted at 6.30 in the evening and the Kreisler team was assigned to Table 6, where an all-male team of students awaited them. This was the second board played at Blum's table:

East-West Game
Dealer West

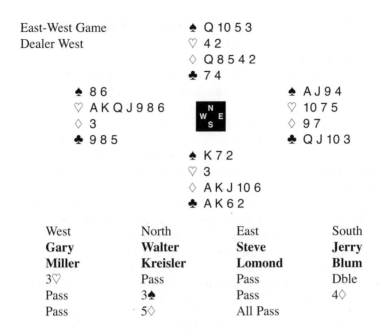

West	North	East	South
Gary	**Walter**	**Steve**	**Jerry**
Miller	**Kreisler**	**Lomond**	**Blum**
3♡	Pass	Pass	Dble
Pass	3♠	Pass	4♢
Pass	5♢	All Pass	

West led the king of hearts and down went the dummy. 'I suppose I have enough to raise,' said Kreisler. 'Five-card trump support, anyway.'

'Great bid,' said Blum. He meant it, too. Many of his clients would pass 4♢ in haste, not realising what a useful hand they had.

Blum ruffed the heart continuation, drew just one round of trumps and played the two top clubs. A club ruff was followed by a trump to his hand and a second club ruff, leaving this end position:

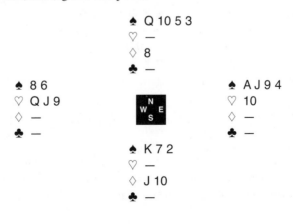

All now depended on the position of the jack of spades. If West held it, a spade to the king could be followed by a finesse of dummy's ten. Blum paused to count the hand. If West held seven hearts for his pre-empt he had started with 7-1-3 shape outside spades, leaving him with only a doubleton spade. The odds therefore favoured playing East for the spade jack. 'Queen of spades, please,' said Blum.

East had to win or Blum would simply lead towards the king on the second round. He then found himself with no good return. Since playing his last heart would concede a fatal ruff-and-discard, he exited with a low spade. Following the odds, Blum ran this to the dummy. He was rewarded by the appearance of a lowly eight from West and the game was made.

'Switch to a spade at Trick 2, Gary!' exclaimed the East player. 'I gave you count on the hearts. You knew another heart wouldn't stand up.'

'Does that make any difference?' his partner asked.

'Of course it does!' came the reply. 'You kill the endplay.'

West returned his cards morosely to the wallet. 'Don't know how I'm supposed to know that,' he said. 'A second heart looked completely safe.'

Three or four boards later, Blum was in game once more.

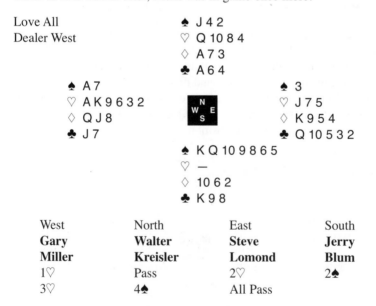

Love All	♠ J 4 2		
Dealer West	♡ Q 10 8 4		
	◇ A 7 3		
	♣ A 6 4		

♠ A 7		♠ 3
♡ A K 9 6 3 2		♡ J 7 5
◇ Q J 8		◇ K 9 5 4
♣ J 7		♣ Q 10 5 3 2

♠ K Q 10 9 8 6 5
♡ —
◇ 10 6 2
♣ K 9 8

West	North	East	South
Gary	**Walter**	**Steve**	**Jerry**
Miller	**Kreisler**	**Lomond**	**Blum**
1♡	Pass	2♡	2♠
3♡	4♠	All Pass	

Miller led the king of hearts and down went the dummy. 'I couldn't decide whether to double 3♡ or raise the spades,' said Walter. 'Hope this is OK.'

'It's fine,' said Blum. 'Small, please.'

Blum ruffed the heart lead and led the king of trumps, taken by West. When the queen of diamonds appeared on the table, he won with dummy's ace. 'Queen of hearts, please,' he said.

Blum threw a diamond loser on the queen of hearts and West won with the heart ace. The jack of diamonds won the next trick and West played a third round of diamonds. Blum ruffed, crossed to dummy with the jack of trumps and and led another heart. Just as he had hoped, the jack appeared from East. He ruffed in the South hand and crossed to the ace of clubs to enjoy a club discard on the established heart ten. The game had been made.

'It's the only lead to give it to him, Gary,' the East player declared. 'Anything else and he has to lose the trump ace and three minor-suit losers.'

The young West player looked wearily across the table. 'You wouldn't lead from an ace-king?' he said.

'Not on this hand,' East replied.

Both pairs in Kreisler's team had performed strongly and a welcome 20-0 win resulted, lifting them into fourth place. The penultimate match, played on Table 2, contained only one board of note:

East-West Game
Dealer South

♠ 10 8 6 5 3 2
♡ J 2
◇ 6 3
♣ Q 7 5

♠ K Q
♡ A Q 10 8
◇ Q J 9 7
♣ 9 8 3

♠ J 9 7 4
♡ 5 3
◇ 10 8 5
♣ K 6 4 2

♠ A
♡ K 9 7 6 4
◇ A K 4 2
♣ A J 10

West	North	East	South
Jimmy	**Jerry**	**Bill**	**Walter**
Yarra	**Blum**	**Lichtman**	**Kreisler**
-	-	-	1♡
Pass	1♠	Pass	3◇
Pass	3♡	Pass	4♡
Dble	All Pass		

Jimmy Yarra, a former body builder whose muscles were now a distant memory, doubled the heart game. There was no further bidding and he led ♠K.

'Not much there for me,' observed Kreisler as the dummy went down.

'No, sorry,' Blum replied. 'I was trying to shut them out.'

Kreisler won the spade lead, cashed two diamonds and ruffed a diamond. When the queen of clubs was covered by the king, he won with the ace. Two more rounds of clubs stood up and he then led his last diamond. West followed suit and East was unable to overruff dummy's jack of trumps. A spade ruff allowed Kreisler to score one of his small trumps and his last four cards were ♠K 9 7 6. He exited with a low trump and eventually scored the king of trumps for his tenth trick. The doubled game had been made.

'Can't you lead a trump, Jimmy?' suggested the East player. 'You stop the diamond ruffs.'

'I wanted to make sure of a spade trick,' his partner replied.

'Lead the ace and queen of trumps and you keep him off the dummy too,' the East player continued. 'He can't take the club finesse. He loses two diamonds, a club and three trump tricks. That's three down!'

Blum leaned forward. 'Only two down, I think,' he said. 'Declarer plays the spade ace and two top diamonds and then exits in diamonds. West cashes two winners in the suit and plays ♠Q, which declarer ruffs. These cards are left...'

Blum scribbled this end position on the back of his scorecard:

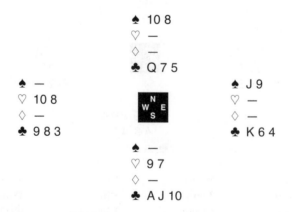

'Yes, yes, it's obvious,' said Yarra. 'He throws me in with the heart and I must play a club. He puts up the queen and it's only two down.'

'There's another twist to it,' said Blum. 'If declarer exits with the seven of trumps, you can win with the ten and return the eight! Now declarer loses a club and a spade. Three down. To prevent this defence, declarer must exit with the nine of trumps rather than the seven.'

Jimmy Yarra had no interest in such lectures. 'It couldn't happen, anyway,' he declared. 'Everyone would lead a spade from my hand.'

The Kreisler team won the match 16-4 and moved into second place, just four points behind the leading team. In their last match they would face the team of the 82-year-old Joshua Heller, an old friend of Kreisler's. Heller did not look too well. His complexion was grey in parts, yellow in others and he held his head at a strange angle. The good news, from his point of view, was that he had looked exactly the same for almost ten years. All rumours of his approaching demise had so far proved wide of the mark.

'You got yourself a better partner than usual?' asked Heller, taking a while to lower himself into the West seat.

'You know Jerry, surely?' Kreisler replied. 'He always makes a trick more than everyone else.'

'Just as well,' Heller retorted. 'Seeing as you always overbid your hand by a trick!'

The players drew their cards for the first board:

```
Game All               ♠ A 5 2
Dealer South           ♡ K Q 10 2
                       ◇ 6 4 3
                       ♣ Q 6 2
        ♠ J 9 8 6                       ♠ 7 3
        ♡ 8                 N           ♡ 6 5 3
        ◇ A K J 10      W       E       ◇ 8 7 2
        ♣ A K 10 8          S           ♣ J 9 7 4 3
                       ♠ K Q 10 4
                       ♡ A J 9 7 4
                       ◇ Q 9 5
                       ♣ 5
```

West	North	East	South
Joshua	**Walter**	**George**	**Jerry**
Heller	**Kreisler**	**Kahn**	**Blum**
-	-	-	1♡
Dble	Rdble	2♣	Pass
3♣	4♡	All Pass	

Heller led the ace of clubs and down went the dummy. 'I pushed it a bit,' said Kreisler. 'If anyone can make ten tricks, you can!'

Blum nodded his thanks for the compliment and surveyed the dummy with no great enthusiasm. What had been the point of the redouble? Holding four-card heart support, Walter surely had no intention of doubling the opponents at a low level. He should have bid 2NT over the double, showing a sound raise to the three-level. 'Nice hand, thanks,' said Blum. 'Play low.'

At Trick 2 Heller switched to the ace of diamonds. East contributed an emphatic two to the trick, looking across at his partner to make sure that the message had been received. No continuation in a side suit was now safe and Heller came off lead with his singleton trump. Blum won in the dummy, ruffed a club in hand and crossed to the king of trumps.

After ruffing dummy's queen of clubs, Blum drew East's last trump and paused to re-assess the situation. Taking two ruffs in his hand had bumped his total to nine tricks – four trumps in the dummy, two ruffs and three top cards in spades. A tenth trick would materialise if the jack of spades fell in three rounds. The odds were against this after West's take-out double and Blum decided to play for another chance. He cashed the king and ace of spades, nothing interesting falling, and these cards remained:

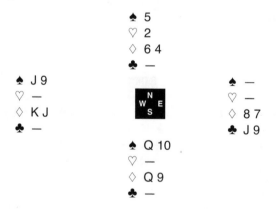

'Play the heart,' said Blum.

He discarded a diamond from his hand and turned to watch the elderly figure to his left. After some thought Heller threw the nine of spades. Blum now cashed the queen and ten of spades for the contract.

Heller grimaced, displaying an expensive set of false teeth. A board like this was not what he wanted on the last round, just when they were in the lead. His health was holding up, yes, but even so there would not be many more years when he would have the chance to win an event like this.

A couple of boards later, Blum was in game again.

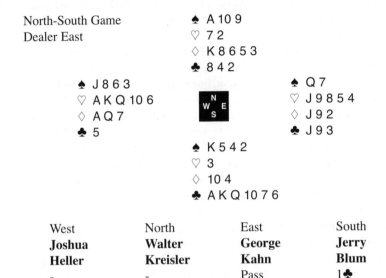

North-South Game
Dealer East

♠ A 10 9
♡ 7 2
◇ K 8 6 5 3
♣ 8 4 2

♠ J 8 6 3
♡ A K Q 10 6
◇ A Q 7
♣ 5

♠ Q 7
♡ J 9 8 5 4
◇ J 9 2
♣ J 9 3

♠ K 5 4 2
♡ 3
◇ 10 4
♣ A K Q 10 7 6

West	North	East	South
Joshua	**Walter**	**George**	**Jerry**
Heller	**Kreisler**	**Kahn**	**Blum**
-	-	Pass	1♣
1♡	Dble	3♡	4♠
Pass	5♣	All Pass	

A negative double of a 1♡ overcall would normally suggest four spades. Kreisler did not have enough for a forcing response of 2◇ and certainly didn't want to raise a possibly short 1♣ opening on three small clubs. Why shouldn't he survive a negative double?

When Blum rebid 4♠ after the pre-emptive heart raise from East, Kreisler was uncertain what to do. It didn't look like the sort of hand on which a 4-3 spade fit would play well. Surely the best chance was to go back to clubs. Partner must have a distributional hand for his bidding.

There was no further bidding over 5♣ and Heller opened the defence with two top hearts. Blum ruffed the second heart and advanced the four of diamonds. It was the key moment of the deal. Heller considered what would happen if he rose with the ace. This might make it easy for declarer to set up the diamonds. He would be able to cross to the king on the second round of the suit and perhaps ruff a third round, finding the suit 3-3. The ace of spades would remain as an entry.

Hoping to kill dummy's diamond suit, Heller followed with the seven of diamonds. Dummy's king won the trick and Blum drew two rounds of trumps, finding that East had started with three cards in the suit. Hoping for the best, he then played a second round of diamonds. Heller won with the diamond queen and had no good card to play. If he played the diamond ace, declarer would ruff and dummy's suit would be set up. Nor would a third round of hearts be any better. Declarer would ruff with dummy's last trump and take advantage of the extra entry by ruffing the diamonds good. No, concluded Heller, he would have to play a spade. Hoping to confuse the position, he exited with a deceptive jack of spades.

Blum now had to read the lie of the spade suit. He was fairly certain of West's holdings outside spades. Had he started with J-x-x-x in the spade suit or Q-J-x-x? The latter holding would give him 18 points and he would have been more likely to start with a take-out double instead of a 1♡ overcall.

Blum ran the jack of spades to his king, drew the outstanding trump and continued with a spade to the ace. The cards lay as he had imagined and East's queen of spades fell to the baize. He ruffed the diamonds good and re-entered dummy with the ten of spades, claiming the contract.

Heller slumped back in his chair, realising that he was not going to win the event. 'At least I made you work for your money,' he said.

It occurred to Blum that West would have done better to play his queen of diamonds on the first round. His partner could then have won the second round, exiting safely with a trump. Still, even a pro might have got that one wrong. 'You sure did,' he replied.

The final match drew to a close and the Kreisler team found that they had won 15-5. The White Pelican Swiss Teams trophy was theirs.

'I am so pleased!' exclaimed Walter Kreisler. 'The only thing that makes me a little bit sad is that we stopped old Joshua from winning it.'

'Ah, don't worry about him,' said Jacob Simmonds. 'He's won plenty of things over the years. Myself, I have never won anything big before.'

'Nor me,' said an excited George Havers. 'How many silver points do we get for such a win? My wife will be so jealous when I tell her!'

The team left the playing area and headed triumphantly into the bar for a celebratory drink. Kreisler drew Jerry to one side. 'You played brilliantly, Jerry,' he said. 'I have added a little bit extra to the cheque, you know, as a small thank you for your efforts.'

Blum nodded appreciatively. 'That's kind of you,' he replied. 'Any time you need me, you know my number.'

'Let's make a date for this event next year, anyway,' declared Kreisler. 'Now, who's for a glass of ice-cold Bud?'

11
Hot Stuff in Florida

The temperature was not far short of a hundred as Blum pulled his blue Taurus into the car park of the Shuffleboard Club in New Port Richey. All the parking spaces in the shade were already taken. He recognised Lindsay Gardner's Corvette in the far corner. Let's hope she didn't try any funny business after the session, he thought. Far too hot for anything like that.

'Hi, you gorgeous hunk,' said Lindsay as Blum entered the club. 'You come straight from the gym?'

'Not exactly,' Blum replied. 'I haven't seen the inside of a gym for a good ten years.'

Lindsay draped a slender arm around Blum's waist. 'How do you keep in such good shape, then?' she asked.

'I do a variety of exercises,' Blum replied. 'Shuffling, dealing, ruffing... that sort of thing.'

Lindsay shrieked with laughter. She was not one to smile or laugh gently. No, the louder she laughed, the greater the sense of humour she demonstrated. That was her opinion, anyway.

The Tuesday and Friday sessions at the Shuffleboard started at 12.30, catering largely for the local retired population. Santa Bennett, the wife of the proprietor, always provided home-made lemon cake and chocolate brownies. Those eager to avail themselves of such freebies were sometimes to be seen queuing outside the club door an hour before play actually started.

'This is my friend, Jerry,' Lindsay announced, as they took their seats for the first round.

Blanche Feldman eyed Lindsay with no great enthusiasm. Didn't she realise that this was a club for retirees? Her sort, forty-year-olds dressed as twenty-year-olds, should be in some neon-lit bar or flaunting themselves on the beach.

This was the first board of the round:

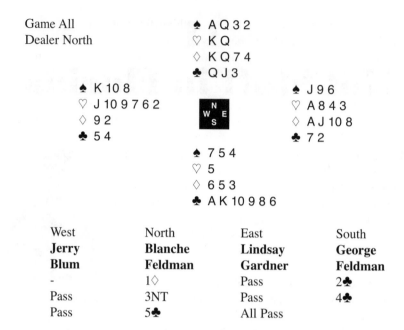

Game All   ♠ A Q 3 2
Dealer North   ♡ K Q
               ◇ K Q 7 4
               ♣ Q J 3

West	North	East	South
Jerry	**Blanche**	**Lindsay**	**George**
Blum	**Feldman**	**Gardner**	**Feldman**
-	1◇	Pass	2♣
Pass	3NT	Pass	4♣
Pass	5♣	All Pass	

The white-haired George Feldman had no justification for disturbing his wife's 3NT. Still, she would doubtless live fifteen years longer than him. It was only right that he should play more than his fair share of hands while he was alive.

Blum led the jack of hearts against the club game and Lindsay won with the ace. When a second heart was returned to dummy's king, Feldman discarded a spade. He then crossed to his hand with a trump and led a diamond to the king. The right defence seemed obvious to Lindsay. She won with the ace and returned the jack of diamonds, clearing the suit.

Feldman came to hand with the ace of trumps and finessed the queen of spades successfully. When he cashed the ace of spades and ruffed a spade high the suit proved to be 3-3. He crossed to dummy with a third round of trumps and threw his diamond loser on the established spade. Eleven tricks had been made.

'Three notrump is easy,' complained Blanche Feldman. 'You have eight top tricks if they lead a heart and a successful spade finesse makes it nine.'

'I couldn't leave it with a singleton heart,' Feldman replied.

Lindsay exchanged a smile with Blum. George was a real shocker. He rarely let his wife play a hand and he rotated about a dozen excuses to justify his outrageous bidding. Too weak to pass 3NT, too strong, too short in hearts, might be a slam on, might be safer in clubs... something different every time. 'Nothing we can do against Five Clubs, is there?' she said.

Blum shrugged his shoulders. 'If I lead a diamond, that beats it,' he replied. 'We can clear the diamonds before he sets up a discard on the hearts.'

Another thought occurred to Blum. Suppose Lindsay had managed a smooth duck of the ace of diamonds. Declarer would then have had no reason to take the spade finesse. He would surely have reckoned it was a better prospect to lead towards the diamond queen. He would need a 3-3 break in the chosen suit either way.

This was the next deal:

East-West Game	♠ A 10 4 3	
Dealer West	♡ A Q 5	
	◇ Q 10 2	
	♣ K Q 6	

♠ Q 8 2	♠ J 9 7 6
♡ J 9 7 6 4	♡ 8 2
◇ —	◇ J 9 8 5 3
♣ J 10 8 5 3	♣ 7 4

♠ K 5
♡ K 10 3
◇ A K 7 6 4
♣ A 9 2

West	North	East	South
Jerry	**Blanche**	**Lindsay**	**George**
Blum	**Feldman**	**Gardner**	**Feldman**
Pass	1NT	Pass	3◇
Pass	3NT	Pass	6◇
All Pass			

Blum led ♣J against the diamond slam and Feldman raised his eyes to the ceiling as the dummy appeared. 'You can't give me seven on that?' he demanded. 'Seventeen points, two aces and queen third of trumps. I bid six missing all those cards and you don't think seven will be a good contract?'

Blanche Feldman reached into her handbag for for a Life Saver mint. Was his sequence invitational? She had not even thought of bidding on. What would George say if she had dared to bid seven and he went one down. He would remind her of the bid for months – every time they played together.

Feldman won the club lead in his hand and cashed the ace of trumps. A smile appeared on his face when Blum discarded a club. 'So lucky you are,' he informed his wife. 'We miss a huge grand and then a bad trump break comes to the rescue.'

'I had a feeling the trumps would break badly,' his wife replied.

Suddenly the smile vanished from Feldman's face. With this 5-0 trump break he was in danger of going down in the small slam! If he played on trumps directly there were two certain losers. The only chance was to turn to the side suits and hope, somehow, that East would have to ruff near the end and lead away from the diamond jack.

Feldman cashed two top spades and ruffed a spade in his hand. He then played two rounds of hearts and a second round of clubs. These cards remained:

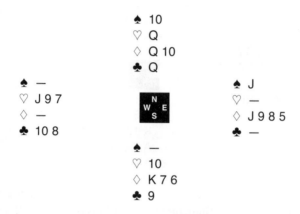

If East's last non-trump card was a heart or a club, the contract could be made at this stage. Declarer would have to remove East's last non-trump, by cashing the right queen, and lead a spade. He could then overruff East's eight or nine with the king and lead his last plain card. East would have to ruff and lead into dummy's Q-10 of trumps.

'Ah, what to do?' exclaimed Feldman. 'So well I have played it but I still need to guess here.'

Eventually he called for the queen of hearts. Lindsay ruffed and exited safely with the jack of spades. She could not be deprived of a further trump trick and the slam went one down.

Blanche Feldman looked towards the ceiling. 'A grand he wanted me to bid!' she exclaimed.

'If trumps are 3-2 the grand is on ice,' Feldman retorted. 'With five trumps over here, I needed an endplay. She is two-two in hearts and clubs. It could not be done.'

Blum said nothing but he realised that declarer had made a mistake as early as Trick 2, on the first round of trumps. Had he led low towards the dummy, he could have picked up a 5-0 break on either side for just one loser. When West showed out, he could win with the queen and lead the ten. The A-K-7-6 over East's J-9-8-5 would restrict her to just one trump trick.

'If the side suits are more friendly, twelve tricks are there on an endplay,' continued George Feldman. 'If the contract could be made I would make it, believe me.'

A round or two later, Blum and Lindsay faced Alan and Santa Bennett, who ran the Shuffleboard Club between them. A larger-than-life couple, their general good humour did much to increase the attendance at the twice weekly sessions.

This was the first board of the round:

```
North-South Game        ♠ 8 7 6 3
Dealer South            ♡ 10 7
                        ◇ A J 3 2
                        ♣ K J 3
         ♠ 5                            ♠ 10 9 2
         ♡ 9 8 2          N             ♡ A K Q 3
         ◇ K 9 8 7 4    W   E           ◇ 6 5
         ♣ 10 7 6 2       S             ♣ A Q 9 4
                        ♠ A K Q J 4
                        ♡ J 6 5 4
                        ◇ Q 10
                        ♣ 8 5
```

West	North	East	South
Jerry	**Alan**	**Lindsay**	**Santa**
Blum	**Bennett**	**Gardner**	**Bennett**
-	-	-	1♠
Pass	3♠	Pass	4♠
All Pass			

The Bennetts had little experience of playing in part scores. When the cards were lying their way, they usually bid to game. Blum led ♡8 and Lindsay won with the queen. Hoping to put her partner on lead for a club return, she switched to a low trump.

Santa Bennett won with the trump ace and surveyed the dummy through her ornate gold spectacles. She drew trumps in two further rounds and then led the queen of diamonds, covered by the king and ace. A diamond back to the ten left this position:

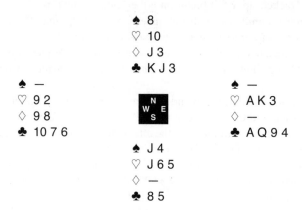

When a heart was played to the ten and king, Lindsay was endplayed. A club return was out of the question, so she tried her luck with the heart ace. Noting that her ♡J was now established, Santa Bennett ruffed in the dummy. She discarded a club on the diamond jack and ten tricks were hers.

Blum maintained an impassive disposition. Hadn't it been obvious to Lindsay that she would be endplayed? If she had cashed a second heart at Trick 2 declarer would have gone down. There would be no way to ruff two hearts and enjoy a third diamond trick. East could ruff the third round of diamonds.

'We should have beaten that,' Lindsay observed.

Blum nodded. It was a bit late but at least she had realised her mistake. Next time she faced a similar situation she would probably get it right.

'You should have led a club, Jerry,' continued Lindsay. 'Ace-queen of clubs, ace-king of hearts. We take the first four tricks!'

This was the next deal:

```
East-West Game              ♠ Q 7 6 4 2
Dealer East                 ♡ K 6 4 3
                            ◇ A J 10
                            ♣ 5
        ♠ A 10 8 3                           ♠ K 9 5
        ♡ 8               ┌─────────┐        ♡ J 2
        ◇ Q 3            │    N    │        ◇ K 8 7 6 5
        ♣ Q J 10 9 7 6   │ W   E   │        ♣ 8 4 2
                          │    S    │
                          └─────────┘
                            ♠ J
                            ♡ A Q 10 9 7 5
                            ◇ 9 4 2
                            ♣ A K 3
```

West	North	East	South
Jerry	**Alan**	**Lindsay**	**Santa**
Blum	**Bennett**	**Gardner**	**Bennett**
-	-	Pass	1♡
2♣	4♣	Pass	4NT
Pass	5♡	Pass	6♡
All Pass			

An extension to the rule that the Bennetts played most part-score deals in game was that they played a fair number of game hands in a slam. Alan Bennett suggested a slam with his splinter bid and his wife resorted immediately to Roman Key-card Blackwood. A few seconds later she was in a small slam.

Blum was aware of the Bennetts' forward bidding style and thought momentarily about leading the spade ace in case they had two top losers in the suit. No, he knew it was the wrong lead. For every time there were two spade tricks to take there would be several occasions where leading the unsupported ace would give away the slam. Hoping for the best, he reached for the queen of clubs.

'Very nice, Alan,' said Santa as the dummy went down. 'Play the five, will you?'

She won the club lead with the ace, crossed to the king of trumps and called for a low spade. Lindsay followed with the five and declarer's jack lost to the ace.

Santa Bennett ruffed Blum's club return and ruffed a spade in her hand. After drawing the last trump, she entered dummy by ruffing the king of clubs. A further spade ruff brought down East's king and the slam was home. Declarer's diamond losers could be thrown on the two established spades in the dummy.

'She shouldn't make that one either, Jerry!' Lindsay exclaimed.

No indeed, thought Blum. Still, it was a difficult shot to rise with the king of spades. It was too much to expect from a client. Even a pro might take the wrong view.

'Lead a diamond and you set up my king,' Lindsay continued. 'When you win with the spade ace we can cash a diamond trick.

'Ah, a diamond lead,' Blum replied. 'That's not easy to find from queen doubleton.'

Lindsay was not overjoyed at suffering two bottoms against Santa Bennett. 'There wasn't much point in a club lead after the splinter bid,' she said. 'I would have led a diamond from your hand.'

The next round took Blum and his partner to the table of one of the weakest pairs in the club. Rarely finishing out of the bottom half, they nevertheless played at various clubs almost every day of the week.

'Hi, Nanci,' said Blum as he took the West seat. 'How're you doing?'

'Not so bad, not so bad,' replied the elderly Nanci Cotrell. 'How's yourself, Jerry?'

'Always a pleasure to play with Lindsay here,' Blum replied, flashing a smile across the table.

'And I always enjoy playing with Bertha, here,' said Nanci. 'Not that we ever do any good.'

'We did OK two Tuesdays ago,' said Bertha Bonetti, who was wearing a thick coat to counter the air conditioning. 'Actually went home with some black points!'

'Only time this year, though,' Nanci added.

The players drew their cards for this deal:

```
Game All              ♠ K 10 8 5 4
Dealer North          ♡ Q 4 2
                      ◇ A Q 3 2
                      ♣ A
   ♠ 9 7                            ♠ A Q J 6 3 2
   ♡ J 10 6 3          N            ♡ A 8
   ◇ 10 9 8 7 5      W   E          ◇ K J 6
   ♣ 9 5               S            ♣ K Q
                      ♠ —
                      ♡ K 9 7 5
                      ◇ 4
                      ♣ J 10 8 7 6 4 3 2
```

West	North	East	South
Jerry	**Bertha**	**Lindsay**	**Nanci**
Blum	**Bonetti**	**Gardner**	**Cotrell**
-	1♠	Pass	2♣
Pass	2◊	Pass	3♣
Pass	3NT	Pass	4♣
Pass	5♣	Dble	All Pass

Nanci gave an exasperated shake of the head as the auction drew to a close. 'No wonder we never do any good when you bid so much!' she exclaimed. 'Two Clubs, Three Clubs... that's a weakness sign-off.'

'That may be but I have a good hand,' Bertha replied.

'You told me that when you bid 3NT,' Nanci continued. 'You must pass Four Clubs, Bertha. That's the most sign-off bid I ever heard.'

Blum led the ten of diamonds and Nanci shook her head again as the modest dummy appeared. 'Win with the ace,' she said.

A diamond ruff drew the jack from East and declarer crossed to the ace of trumps to ruff another diamond. This time the king appeared from Lindsay in the East seat. When Nanci played a second round of trumps, Lindsay won with the king and paused to contemplate her return. Although only five tricks had passed, she was endplayed. Ace and another heart would give declarer two heart tricks and an entry to dummy's established ◊Q. It seemed better to play the ace of spades. Even if this was ruffed, declarer might not be able to find her way to dummy.

Nanci ruffed the ace of spades and surveyed the two winners in dummy – the king of spades and the diamond queen. How could she reach them? A heart towards the queen would work if West held the ace of hearts. Unfortunately, East's double suggested that she held that card. Suddenly inspiration struck her. Of course! The king of hearts would force out the ace. Then she could cross to the queen of hearts.

A small flaw in this plan was exposed when the king of hearts was allowed to win the trick. Nanci continued with a second heart towards the queen, West playing low. What now? Surely Jerry would have risen with the ace if he held it, she thought. It must be obvious to him, otherwise, that dummy's queen would win and she would discard her remaining heart losers for a doubled overtrick. 'Play the four,' she said.

Lindsay reluctantly produced the ace and the doubled game had been made. 'There was nothing wrong with my double,' Lindsay declared. 'I had a 2NT opener!'

'Yes, my opening lead wasn't the best,' Blum replied. 'A trump lead kills an entry to dummy. Nanci couldn't eliminate your diamonds.'

Nanci smiled at Blum, patting him on the hand. 'You took pity on an old lady,' she said.

A round or two later, Blum and his partner arrived at the table of the best pair in the club, Joe Garcia and Eddie Rodolfo. Despite having no visible form of employment, Garcia lived in a 20-room marble mansion with a private lake. Most club members gave him the benefit of the doubt and assumed he had inherited his money.

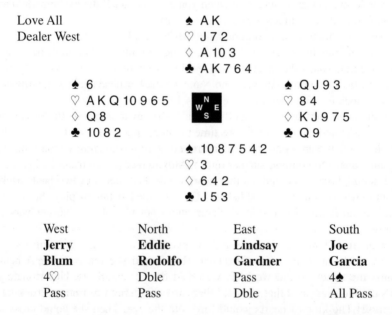

Love All
Dealer West

♠ A K
♡ J 7 2
◇ A 10 3
♣ A K 7 6 4

♠ 6
♡ A K Q 10 9 6 5
◇ Q 8
♣ 10 8 2

♠ Q J 9 3
♡ 8 4
◇ K J 9 7 5
♣ Q 9

♠ 10 8 7 5 4 2
♡ 3
◇ 6 4 2
♣ J 5 3

West	North	East	South
Jerry	**Eddie**	**Lindsay**	**Joe**
Blum	**Rodolfo**	**Gardner**	**Garcia**
4♡	Dble	Pass	4♠
Pass	Pass	Dble	All Pass

Blum played two top hearts and the sun-tanned declarer ruffed the second round. After a trump to the ace he cashed the ace-king of clubs, nodding his approval when the queen appeared. 'Play a small club, Eddie,' he said.

Lindsay surveyed the scene uncertainly. It wasn't right to ruff, was it? If Jerry had the club jack, her two trump tricks would put the contract at least one down. It would look stupid to ruff partner's club winner with a natural trump trick.

Lindsay discarded a diamond and declarer's jack of clubs won the trick. When a second round of trumps was played to dummy's king Blum showed out. 'Play a club,' said Garcia.

There was no longer any defence. Whether or not Lindsay chose to ruff, declarer would throw his two diamond losers on dummy's good clubs. The doubled game had been made.

Garcia turned scornfully to his right. 'You should ruff the third club, lady,' he said. 'Then you switch to a diamond and I can't get both my losers away in time.'

'I didn't know where the jack of clubs was,' Lindsay replied. 'I wouldn't want to switch away from the king of diamonds, anyway. You might hold the queen.'

Garcia gave a dismissive shake of the head. 'You want to beat the contract, that's what you must do,' he said.

Blum was not enchanted by his opponent's manners but it was not his style to make enemies at the table. For all he knew, the man might be in need of a professional partner one day. Potential clients with a mansion and a private lake were not so easy to find. 'Clever point, Joe,' he observed. 'Still, it was a difficult defence.'

Lindsay smiled gratefully at Blum. 'If it would be difficult for you, what chance did poor little me have?' she said.

The session drew to a close and Blum was soon walking out into the blazing sunshine again. If anything it was hotter than when he had arrived.

Lindsay reached playfully for her cheque-book. 'Shall I make it out for the usual amount?' she said.

'That'll be fine,' Blum replied. 'Thanks.'

'Or... er...' Lindsay smiled flirtatiously, 'would you like to come back to my place?'

Amorous encounters with clients had cost Blum his second marriage. Lucille had never understood that that they were just part of his job. He had no wife to worry about now of course and... well, it hadn't been a very good month financially.

'I was hoping you'd say that,' Blum replied, pressing the remote-unlock of his Taurus. 'Race you back to your place!'

12
A Glimpse of Heaven

Jerry Blum and Bob Schafer surveyed the scene at London's White House Hotel where the Macallan International Pairs was about to start. There was a lavish hospitality room, with the sponsor's 10-year-old malt on offer as well as a wide selection of canapés on silver trays. The large VuGraph theatre would seat some four hundred spectators and there were several playing rooms, each accommodating one or two tables and around fifty kibitzers. The prize money might not be huge but it was one of the most glamorous events of the year. Sixteen of the world's best pairs had been invited and for the first time... Blum and Schafer were among them!

There would be no easy opponents in such an event and the first round saw the Americans facing Zia Mahmood and Andrew Robson. An army of kibitzers pressed around them as play began. After faring somewhat poorly on a couple of part score deals, Blum arrived in a small slam.

Love All
Dealer West

	♠ A Q 7 4	
	♡ 6 4	
	◇ J 9 7 6	
	♣ A 6 4	
♠ —		♠ K 10 9 8 6 5
♡ J 9 3 2	N W E S	♡ Q 10 8
◇ 3 2		◇ 8 5 4
♣ K Q J 10 8 7 3		♣ 2
	♠ J 3 2	
	♡ A K 7 5	
	◇ A K Q 10	
	♣ 9 5	

West	North	East	South
Robson	**Schafer**	**Mahmood**	**Blum**
3♣	Pass	Pass	Dble
Pass	4♣	Pass	4◇
Pass	5◇	Pass	6◇
All Pass			

Schafer did not like to cue-bid the club ace over 4◇. He was minimum for his original cue-bid response and his trumps were only jack-high. Blum advanced to the small slam nevertheless and the king of clubs was led. 'Thanks, Bob,' he said, relieved to find that there were not two top club losers. 'Play the ace.'

Blum drew one round of trumps with the ace and then cashed the two top hearts. A heart ruff in dummy was followed by a second round of trumps to the king and a heart ruff with the bare jack, East discarding a spade. These cards remained:

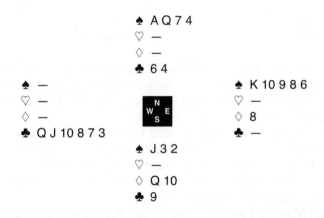

```
                    ♠ A Q 7 4
                    ♡ —
                    ◇ —
                    ♣ 6 4
    ♠ —                              ♠ K 10 9 8 6
    ♡ —                              ♡ —
    ◇ —                              ◇ 8
    ♣ Q J 10 8 7 3                   ♣ —
                    ♠ J 3 2
                    ♡ —
                    ◇ Q 10
                    ♣ 9
```

West's initial shape had been exposed as 0-4-2-7 and Blum could see that he would make the contract. 'Small spade, please,' he said.

If Zia played the spade king on thin air, declarer would make three spade tricks for the contract. He played low instead and Blum won with the spade jack. After drawing East's last trump, he played another spade and ducked in the dummy. Zia gave a resigned nod of the head and returned his cards to the wallet. The slam had been made.

'Sorry,' said Robson. 'If I don't open they wouldn't get there.'

Zia smiled at his partner. 'This time I'll forgive you,' he replied.

A board or two later, Blum arrived in Four Hearts.

Game All   ♠ A Q
Dealer South   ♡ A 10 5 2
                 ◊ Q 9 5 4 2
                 ♣ 10 3

♠ 6		♠ J 7 5 4 2
♡ Q 9 3	**N**	♡ 7
◊ A 6 3	**W** **E**	◊ K J 10 8
♣ K Q J 9 8 6	**S**	♣ 7 5 4

                 ♠ K 10 9 8 3
                 ♡ K J 8 6 4
                 ◊ 7
                 ♣ A 2

West	North	East	South
Robson	**Schafer**	**Mahmood**	**Blum**
-	-	-	1♠
2♣	2◊	Pass	2♡
Pass	4♡	All Pass	

Blum won the ♣K lead and played a trump to the ace. What now?

The right play was surely to finesse the jack of trumps, thought Blum. If this lost to a doubleton queen there would be two trumps left in dummy to deal with the potential spade losers. 'Play a trump,' he said.

It was an unpleasant surprise when East showed out. Blum won with the trump king and played the ace and queen of spades. All would have been well if West had ruffed with the master queen of trumps. Andrew Robson had no intention of doing this, however, since he could use the card to draw two trumps for one if he gained the lead later.

When Blum led a diamond from dummy, Zia won with the eight and crossed to his partner's hand with a club. After drawing a third round of trumps, Robson played the diamond ace. Blum ruffed in the South hand but he was a trick short and could not avoid going one down.

'Tough breaks,' said Schafer, gathering up the dummy's cards and returning them to the wallet. What was Jerry thinking of? A diamond at Trick 2, to establish communications, and the contract would have been cold. He could draw a second round of trumps and continue unimpeded with the cross-ruff.

Blum shook his head in rueful fashion. 'I should have played a diamond earlier,' he said.

In the Macallan Pairs each result was IMPed against a datum, the average score from all the tables. The total IMP difference in a match was then converted into Victory Points. Blum and Schafer found they had won their first match 27-23. Not a bad start but it could have been so much better.

The second round saw them facing the French stars, Paul Chemla and Christian Mari. Terence Reese once famously wrote of Chemla: He is reputed to frequent all the best restaurants in Paris, a claim to which his appearance lends support. Blum fixed the chandelier-lit scene in his memory. What an experience to face one world-famous pair after another! To end in a good position would just be a bonus.

Mari made an easy 3NT on the first board. This was the second:

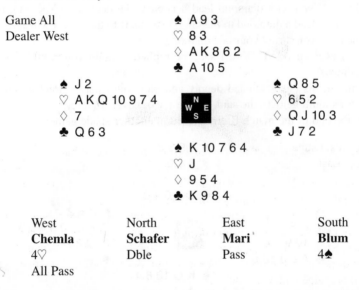

Game All	♠ A 9 3
Dealer West	♡ 8 3
	◇ A K 8 6 2
	♣ A 10 5

♠ J 2		♠ Q 8 5
♡ A K Q 10 9 7 4		♡ 6 5 2
◇ 7		◇ Q J 10 3
♣ Q 6 3		♣ J 7 2

	♠ K 10 7 6 4
	♡ J
	◇ 9 5 4
	♣ K 9 8 4

West	North	East	South
Chemla	**Schafer**	**Mari**	**Blum**
4♡	Dble	Pass	4♠
All Pass			

Blum arrived in Four Spades and Chemla launched the defence with two top hearts, East signalling an odd number of cards in the suit. Blum ruffed the second round and played a trump to the ace. He then cashed the ace of diamonds and led a second round of trumps. When the eight appeared from East he finessed the ten, losing to the jack.

If Chemla had held another diamond, the suit would have broken 3-2 and provided two discards for the clubs. As the cards lay, the Frenchman had no diamond left and was endplayed. A third round of hearts would allow declarer to ruff with dummy's last trump, throwing a diamond loser from his hand. After a few seconds thought Chemla flipped the queen of clubs on to the table.

Blum paused to calculate the likely lie of the club suit. If Chemla did indeed have no cards remaining in spades and diamonds, his shape would be 2-7-1-3. There were twelve possible Q-x-x and J-x-x holdings and only four Q-J-x holdings. It followed that when West exited with a club honour (it made no difference which) the odds were 3-to-1 in favour of him holding one honour rather than two. 'Play the ace,' said Blum.

After drawing the last trump, Blum led a second round of diamonds, West showing out as expected. He then had to rely on the clubs. A finesse through East succeeded and when the suit broke 3-3, as Blum's count of the hand had suggested, the contract was made.

Chemla opened a small knife and cut the end off one of his trade-mark Monte Cristo cigars. 'Even on a diamond lead it is easy,' he declared. 'You win, play trump ace-king, lead a diamond to the king, then heart to the jack. I win and cash another heart... you throw your last diamond!'

Blum's eyes sparkled. 'Yes, I see,' he replied. 'Again you would have to open the clubs.'

Chemla lit his cigar, inhaled deeply and blew out a large cloud of smoke. 'The datum should be 620,' he said, 'but you can never be sure.'

Near the end of the match Blum arrived in another spade game:

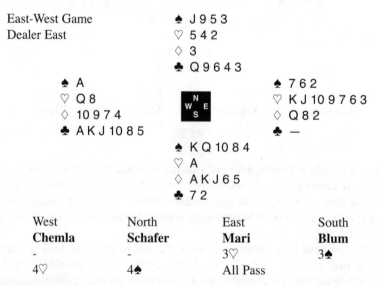

West	North	East	South
Chemla	**Schafer**	**Mari**	**Blum**
-	-	3♡	3♠
4♡	4♠	All Pass	

Chemla led the king of clubs, drawing a discard of ◇2 from his partner. When he continued with the club ace, Mari threw ◇8. The jack of clubs was led to Trick 3, covered by dummy's queen.

Christian Mari paused to consider his defence. Suppose he ruffed this trick and declarer followed suit. What would be the fourth trick for the defence? If West held ◊A or a cashable ♡A, he would surely have played it before delivering the club ruff. Since Chemla had not cashed a red ace, it seemed that declarer must hold them both. In that case the best chance for the defence was that Chemla held the ace of trumps.

His mind made up, Mari discarded his last diamond. The contract was now doomed. When Blum played on trumps, Chemla won with the ace and delivered a diamond ruff.

Shafer looked respectfully at the two Frenchmen. 'Nice defence,' he observed.

Chemla celebrated with a deep draw on his cigar. 'If I had a red ace I would cash it,' he said.

Blum and Schafer were surprised to find they had lost their second match quite heavily, by 16-34 in victory points, and were now lying only eleventh out of the sixteen pairs. 'We didn't do much wrong there, did we?' said Schafer. 'The datums all seemed to go against us.'

The next string of matches went better for the American pair and they were in fourth place as they took their seats for the last match of the day. Their opponents would be the Germans, Sabine Auken and Daniela von Arnim, who had some claim to be the top ladies pair in the world.

Game All		♠ A 9 7 5	
Dealer East		♡ 3	
		◊ A K 6 4	
		♣ J 6 5 3	

♠ 8 6 4		♠ K Q J 10 3
♡ 8 6 5 2	N W E S	♡ A 4
◊ Q 9 8 5		◊ J 10 3
♣ K 8		♣ Q 10 7

	♠ 2	
	♡ K Q J 10 9 7	
	◊ 7 2	
	♣ A 9 4 2	

West	North	East	South
von Arnim	**Shafer**	**Auken**	**Blum**
-	-	1♠	2♡
Pass	2NT	Pass	4♡
All Pass			

A spade was led and Blum won with the ace in dummy. The game seemed a comfortable one but he could see that there might be a problem with keeping control if trumps broke 4-2.

A trump to the king won the second trick and he continued with the queen of trumps from his hand. Despite what most of the kibitzers might have thought, the discard from dummy was critical. All of dummy's spades would be needed and Blum decided to throw a diamond. The blonde-haired Auken won with the trump ace and forced declarer with a spade. Blum ruffed and drew West's remaining trumps, throwing a club and another diamond from the dummy. He was now left with just one trump in his hand. How could he set up a long card in clubs without losing control? These cards remained:

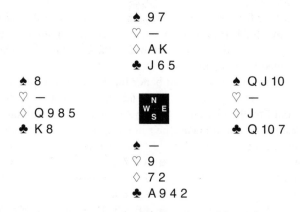

```
                    ♠ 9 7
                    ♡ —
                    ◇ A K
                    ♣ J 6 5
    ♠ 8                              ♠ Q J 10
    ♡ —              ┌───────┐       ♡ —
    ◇ Q 9 8 5        │  N    │       ◇ J
    ♣ K 8            │ W   E │       ♣ Q 10 7
                     │   S   │
                     └───────┘
                    ♠ —
                    ♡ 9
                    ◇ 7 2
                    ♣ A 9 4 2
```

When Blum led a low club from his hand, Daniela von Arnim had a difficult decision to make in the West seat. She chose to rise with the king of clubs and force declarer's last trump with another round of spades. This defence did not pay off. After ruffing the spade, Blum cashed dummy's two top diamonds. To keep the clubs guarded, East had to reduce to the bare queen of spades. She was thrown in with that card on the next trick and had to lead away from the queen of clubs. Had Blum not retained every one of the dummy's spades, the throw-in would not have been possible.

'Great play, Jerry!' exclaimed Shafer. If the match continued in this vein they would be close to the lead overnight.

Daniela von Arnim looked anxiously across the table. 'Is it better if I play low on the club?' she asked. 'You can win and force his last trump.'

'I don't think so,' her partner replied. 'He can duck the second round of clubs to your king. You wouldn't have any spades left.'

'That's right,' said Blum 'I don't have the option of ace and another club, hoping to lose the third round to West, because there would be no entry to my long club.'

A board or two later, with the time edging towards midnight, the spotlight was on Blum again.

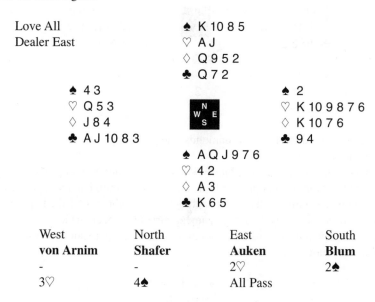

Love All
Dealer East

♠ K 10 8 5
♡ A J
◇ Q 9 5 2
♣ Q 7 2

♠ 4 3
♡ Q 5 3
◇ J 8 4
♣ A J 10 8 3

♠ 2
♡ K 10 9 8 7 6
◇ K 10 7 6
♣ 9 4

♠ A Q J 9 7 6
♡ 4 2
◇ A 3
♣ K 6 5

West	North	East	South
von Arnim	**Shafer**	**Auken**	**Blum**
-	-	2♡	2♠
3♡	4♠	All Pass	

West led ♡3 against the spade game and Blum nodded his thanks as the dummy was laid out. The best chance for a make seemed to be to find West with the king of diamonds. In that case he would be able to set up a discard for one of his club losers. Still, there was no rush to go in with the ace of hearts. If West did hold the diamond king, there was no way that East would be able to set up two club tricks before it was dislodged.

Blum kept his options open by playing the jack of hearts at Trick 1. Sabine Auken won with the king and returned ♣9. Blum digested the implications of this. Surely West held the club ace and East was therefore a strong favourite to hold the king of diamonds. In that case, he would need an endplay on East to make the game.

Blum rose with the king of clubs at Trick 2, aiming to break the link between the two defenders. West won with the ace and returned the jack of clubs, removing dummy's queen. Blum drew trumps in two rounds and cashed the ace of diamonds, leaving these cards still to be played:

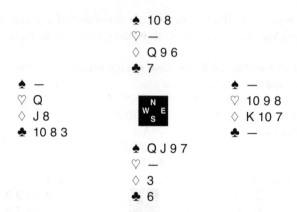

```
              ♠ 10 8
              ♡ —
              ◇ Q 9 6
              ♣ 7
♠ —                        ♠ —
♡ Q           N            ♡ 10 9 8
◇ J 8       W   E          ◇ K 10 7
♣ 10 8 3      S            ♣ —
              ♠ Q J 9 7
              ♡ —
              ◇ 3
              ♣ 6
```

When Blum led the three of diamonds, the eight appeared from West. 'Play the nine,' he said.

Sabine Auken could see her fate. With a resigned nod she won with the ten and played the king of diamonds. Blum ruffed in the South hand and crossed to dummy with a trump to discard his club loser on the established queen of diamonds. Yet another touch-and-go game contract had been made.

The next few hands went well enough for the American pair and Blum then picked up this moderate collection:

```
♠ Q J 7 4 3
♡ 10 7 5
◇ 9 6 4
♣ 7 3
```

Von Arnim, sitting West, opened 1♣. The German women played the Precision Club system and this opening bid was artificial, promising at least 16 points. Shafer passed and after a negative 1◇ response from the German East, von Arnim rebid 2◇. Shafer sprung to life with a take-out double, which at Game All suggested a fair hand. Auken jumped to 4◇ and Blum looked once more at his moderate collection. Only three points, it was true, but partner would be very short in diamonds and should hold several good cards elsewhere. Blum reached into his bidding box for the 4♠ card.

The German West passed and Shafer raised to 6♠. Blum maintained a passive expression. Wow! They had bid a slam after an adverse strong club opening. This proved to be the full deal:

Game All   ♠ A K 6 5
Dealer West   ♡ A K J 9 8
                        ◊ —
                        ♣ K 10 8 2

	♠ 8		♠ 10 9 2
	♡ Q 6 2	N	♡ 4 3
	◊ A K Q 8 7	W E	◊ J 10 6 3 2
	♣ A Q 9 5	S	♣ J 6 4

                  ♠ Q J 7 4 3
                  ♡ 10 7 5
                  ◊ 9 5 4
                  ♣ 7 3

West	North	East	South
von Arnim	**Shafer**	**Auken**	**Blum**
1♣	Pass	1◊	Pass
2◊	Dble	4◊	4♠
Pass	6♣	All Pass	

Blum ruffed the diamond lead in dummy and drew two rounds of trumps with the ace and queen. If the trumps had broken 2-2, he would have finessed in hearts next. A successful finesse would allow him to throw two clubs on the hearts and eventually return to hand with a club ruff in order to ruff another diamond.

When the trumps broke 3-1 Blum calculated that he would need to find the ace of clubs onside. Since there were only 19 points out and West had opened with a strong club, this was a near certainty. When he led a low club from his hand the German West rose with the ace and exited with the six of hearts. Committed to a finesse in that suit, Blum ran the heart switch to his ten. East followed impotently with a low card and the slam was his.

'Queen-jack fifth and nothing?' queried Shafer. 'Good bid.'

The session drew to a close and the players withdrew to the hospitality room. Blum had never been happier. Here they were, surrounded by the best players on the planet. Not only that, they were rising ever higher in the ranking list. Whatever happened tomorrow, on the final day's play, he would remember this event for ever.

13
Brazilian Slams

With thirty minutes to go before the start of the final day's play, Blum and Shafer stood proudly in front of the leader board. Sixteen pairs were competing and these were the leading six positions:

1.	Helgemo and Helness (Norway)	332
2.	Lauria and Versace (Italy)	319
3.	Blum and Shafer (USA)	307
4.	Meckstroth and Rodwell (USA)	302
5.	Mahmood and Robson (USA/England)	290
6.	Chagas and Branco (Brazil)	272

Such a placing, among the world's best, was way beyond the American pair's initial expectations. Ahead of Eric and Jeff! There were still five rounds to go, of course, and it would be easy to slip down the list. Even so, it was a moment to be savoured.

Blum and Shafer suffered a narrow loss in their first match, against a Polish pair. They had dropped one place, into fourth position, as they took their seats against the leaders – Geir Helgemo and Tor Helness of Norway. This match was to be played on VuGraph and, with tickets having been sold out two weeks before the event, the theatre was packed.

The diagram for the first board of the match was displayed on the large VuGraph screen:

Shafer

Love All
Dealer North

♠ A 7 3
♡ A K Q J 10
◇ K 7 3
♣ A 2

Helgemo

♠ 8 5 2
♡ 6 5 2
◇ Q 6 4
♣ K Q J 9

Helness

♠ K Q J 10 4
♡ 9 8 7 3
◇ A 5
♣ 6 4

Blum

♠ 9 6
♡ 4
◇ J 10 9 8 2
♣ 10 8 7 5 3

'Nice hand for Shafer in the North seat,' said Barry Rigal, who was one of the world's top VuGraph commentators. An Englishman by birth, he now lived with his American wife in New York. 'Four Hearts would go several down, though, and game in notrumps is also hopeless.'

'They might make Five Diamonds,' observed his fellow commentator, Canada's Eric Kokish. 'Very difficult to reach, though.'

'NORTH: One Heart,' called the female announcer's shrill voice, which was being relayed from the playing room. 'EAST: One Spade, SOUTH: Pass, West: Two Spades.'

'What will North say now, do you think, Barry?' asked Kokish. 'Two notrump?'

'NORTH: Double,' intervened the announcer. 'EAST: Pass, SOUTH: Three Diamonds, WEST: Pass.'

'Ah, they've found the diamonds!' exclaimed Rigal.

'NORTH: Three Hearts, EAST: Pass.'

'Tempting for South to pass now,' Kokish observed. 'If he finds Four Clubs, the Americans could be in business.'

'SOUTH: Four Clubs, WEST: Pass, NORTH: Five Diamonds,' continued the announcer. 'EAST: Pass, SOUTH: Pass, WEST: Pass. The final contract is Five Diamonds by South.'

Unheard by the players in the sound-proof playing room, there was a smattering of applause from the VuGraph audience.

'Of course he hasn't made it yet,' said Rigal. 'In fact, it may be quite difficult to arrive at eleven tricks. If dummy is forced in clubs declarer can't pick up the queen of trumps.'

'Opening lead is the king of clubs,' declared the announcer.

'I think he has to duck this,' said Kokish. 'Otherwise dummy will be forced when East takes his ace of trumps.

'NORTH: two of clubs, EAST: six of clubs, SOUTH: three of clubs.'

'He's over the first hurdle,' said Rigal. 'It's a tricky hand. I think he may need some fancy work in the trump suit, to be able to get back to dummy's top hearts.'

Helgemo played a second club at Trick 2, won with dummy's ace. Blum cashed two rounds of hearts, throwing a spade, and continued with the ace of spades. As Rigal had predicted, he then ruffed a spade with the eight of trumps, retaining the trump two. The jack of trumps was run to the East's ace and, thanks to the hold-up at Trick 1, Helness had no club with which to force the dummy. When he returned a spade, Blum ruffed with the nine. These cards remained:

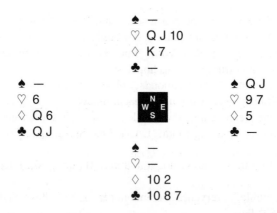

```
              ♠ —
              ♡ Q J 10
              ◇ K 7
              ♣ —
♠ —                        ♠ Q J
♡ 6        ┌─────┐         ♡ 9 7
◇ Q 6      │ N   │         ◇ 5
♣ Q J      │W   E│         ♣ —
           │  S  │
           └─────┘
              ♠ —
              ♡ —
              ◇ 10 2
              ♣ 10 8 7
```

Rigal moved the microphone to his lips. 'Just one trap left,' he said. 'If declarer tries to play the two of trumps to the seven, Helgemo can put in the queen to kill the entry.'

'He will be there with the queen, believe me,' added Kokish.

'SOUTH: Ten of diamonds,' came the high-pitched voice of the announcer.

It now made no difference which trump Helgemo played in the West seat. When he chose to cover, Blum won with the king and drew West's last trump with the seven. Dummy was high and the contract had been made. The audience in the VuGraph room burst into applause.

'I think we can see why Blum and Shafer are in fourth position,' said Barry

Rigal. 'Fine technique by declarer, there.'

There was little action on the next few deals and the VuGraph commentators had to earn their money, keeping the spectators entertained. With three deals remaining, this lay-out flashed onto the VuGraph screen:

North-South Game
Dealer South

Shafer
♠ A 9 6 5
♡ K J 2
◇ 8 7 3
♣ A 7 2

Helgemo
♠ Q 10 7 2
♡ —
◇ J 5 4 2
♣ J 9 8 6 5

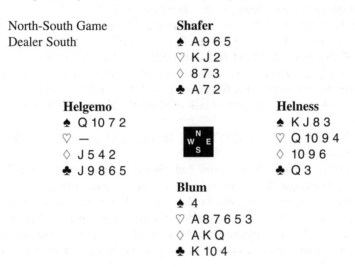

Helness
♠ K J 8 3
♡ Q 10 9 4
◇ 10 9 6
♣ Q 3

Blum
♠ 4
♡ A 8 7 6 5 3
◇ A K Q
♣ K 10 4

'A borderline slam for the Americans,' said Rigal. 'There's a loser in clubs, so you need to pick up the trumps.'

'Single queen or a 2-2 break,' said Kokish. 'It's a fraction above fifty percent but, as we can see, the trumps lie very badly.'

'I think there may be a double-dummy make,' observed Rigal. 'You can ruff three spades and cash the winners in the minors. East would then have to ruff at Trick 10 and lead into the trump tenace.'

'SOUTH: One Heart,' declared the announcer. 'WEST: Pass, NORTH: One Spade, EAST: Pass.'

'If South rebids Three Hearts now, I expect they'll bid the slam,' Rigal predicted. 'The heart suit is poor, though. He might prefer Two Diamonds.'

'SOUTH: Three Hearts, WEST: Pass, NORTH: Four Clubs, East: Pass.'

'It's more sensible to play Four Clubs as a cue-bid rather than natural,' Kokish informed the audience. 'That's what the Americans play and I dare say all of the other pairs here too.'

SOUTH: Four Diamonds, WEST: Pass, NORTH: Four Spades, EAST: Pass.'

'South may still be worried about the trump suit,' said Rigal. 'Partner could hold honour doubleton on this bidding. 'I expect he'll bid Five Diamonds now and leave any further move to his partner.'

'SOUTH: Six Hearts, WEST: Pass, NORTH: Pass, EAST: Pass. The final contract is Six Hearts by South.'

'Well at least that proves Blum isn't looking at East's hand!' quipped Kokish. 'Do you think there's any chance of the slam being made?'

'West leads the seven of spades,' continued the announcer. 'NORTH: ace of spades, EAST: three of spades, SOUTH: four of spades.'

'The Norwegians play third and fifth leads, as we have seen on the other boards,' said Rigal. 'Declarer may take the view that nothing is lost by ruffing a spade, beginning the preparation for an end-play. If East holds queen third in the trump suit, along with the queen and jack of clubs, there would be the chance of endplaying him in clubs.'

'NORTH: five of spades, EAST: king of spades, SOUTH: three of hearts, WEST: two of spades.'

Over in the playing room, Blum had folded his cards and was leaning forward deep in thought. There was no reason whatsoever to finesse West for the queen of trumps. Since he intended to play for the drop in trumps, he might as well use the king of trumps as an entry for a further spade ruff. The spades appeared to be 4-4 and by eliminating the spades he would have the option of attempting to endplay East in clubs if he judged that he had started with three trumps.

When Blum played a trump to the king, West showed out. It was bad news in a way but it meant also that Blum's early preparation might bear fruit. He ruffed another spade, crossed to the ace of clubs and ruffed dummy's last spade. All followed to the king of clubs and the two top diamonds, leaving these cards still to be played:

Shafer
♠ —
♡ J 2
◇ 8
♣ 7

Helgemo
♠ —
♡ —
◇ J 5
♣ J 9 8

Helness
♠ —
♡ Q 10 9
◇ 9
♣ —

```
    N
  W   E
    S
```

Blum
♠ —
♡ A 8
◇ Q
♣ 10

'There's no guess involved,' said Eric Kokish. 'If East's last non-trump card is the jack of clubs, the slam cannot be made. Declarer could exit in clubs and force a lead from the trump queen but he would still have a second loser.'

'SOUTH: Queen of diamonds, WEST: five of diamonds, NORTH: eight of diamonds, EAST: nine of diamonds,' said the announcer. 'SOUTH: ten of clubs...'

'He's made it!' said Rigal. 'Another excellent board for the Americans.' He glanced down at the result slips from the other tables. 'Five other pairs bid the slam but no-one else made it. Blum and Shafer seem to be heading for a fair-sized win in this match.'

Blum and Shafer defeated the Norwegians 34-16 and scored a narrow win in their next match, against a Russian pair. With two rounds to go, they were lying in a magnificent third place. Their next opponents would be USA's mighty Meckstroth and Rodwell, who were performing strongly and had moved into second place, only 3 VPs behind the Norwegians. An army of kibitzers were packed around the table as the players took their seats for this key encounter.

There was little action on the first few boards. Meckstroth then arrived in game on this board:

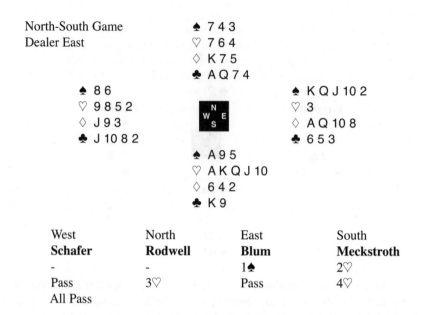

North-South Game
Dealer East

♠ 7 4 3
♡ 7 6 4
◇ K 7 5
♣ A Q 7 4

♠ 8 6
♡ 9 8 5 2
◇ J 9 3
♣ J 10 8 2

♠ K Q J 10 2
♡ 3
◇ A Q 10 8
♣ 6 5 3

♠ A 9 5
♡ A K Q J 10
◇ 6 4 2
♣ K 9

West	North	East	South
Schafer	**Rodwell**	**Blum**	**Meckstroth**
-	-	1♠	2♡
Pass	3♡	Pass	4♡
All Pass			

Schafer led ♣8 against the heart game, Blum contributing the ten. The kibitzers at Meckstroth's elbow were surprised to see him duck this trick. What possible purpose could there be in that?

Meckstroth won the spade continuation and drew trumps in four rounds. He then played three rounds of clubs to reach this end position:

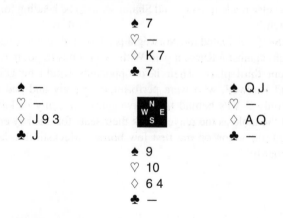

♠ 7
♡ —
◇ K 7
♣ 7

♠ —
♡ —
◇ J 9 3
♣ J

♠ Q J
♡ —
◇ A Q
♣ —

♠ 9
♡ 10
◇ 6 4
♣ —

152

'Play the club,' said Meckstroth.

Blum considered his discard carefully. If he threw a spade, declarer would ruff the club and exit in spades, forcing him to concede a trick to dummy's king of diamonds. That was no good. The only alternative was to throw the diamond queen.

When the diamond queen appeared, Meckstroth discarded the last spade from his hand. He now reaped the benefit from his duck in spades at Trick 1. With only diamonds in his hand, West had to return a diamond. Meckstroth played low from dummy and the bare ace appeared from East. Dummy's ◇K was good and the contract had been made.

It was not the habit of Meckstroth and Rodwell to congratulate each other but for a second their eyes met. Rodwell gave a small nod, acknowledging the fine effort of his partner.

'I beat it if I lead the jack or nine of diamonds,' observed Schafer. 'No way I'm going to find that.'

Blum and Shafer performed satisfactorily on a bunch of part score deals. Jeff Meckstroth then arrived in a slam.

North-South Game	♠ A J 10 9 4	
Dealer East	♡ A 6	
	◇ A 3	
	♣ A J 6 3	

♠ 6 3 2		♠ 8
♡ 5	N W E S	♡ Q 10 9 8 7 3
◇ Q 9 8 6 4 2		◇ J 10 5
♣ Q 8 5		♣ K 9 7

♠ K Q 7 5
♡ K J 4 2
◇ K 7
♣ 10 4 2

West	North	East	South
Schafer	**Rodwell**	**Blum**	**Meckstroth**
-	-	2♡	Pass
Pass	Dble	Pass	4♠
Pass	6♠	All Pass	

It is one of Meckstroth and Rodwell's theories that after a protective double you should not choose to defend with only four trumps. With the vulnerability as it was, Meckstroth gave no thought at all to defending. He leapt to the spade game and was surprised to see his partner raise to a small slam.

Praying that Blum might hold the heart ace, Schafer led his singleton in the suit. The appearance of dummy dispelled this hope. Meckstroth thought for some time before playing to the first trick. 'Play the ace,' he said eventually.

Even though East was non-vulnerable it seemed likely that he would hold at least one of the missing club honours. After drawing trumps in three rounds, Meckstroth led a low club from the dummy. If Blum rose with the king he would set up a finesse against partner's queen. He played low with no hint of a hesitation and declarer's ten lost to West's queen. The club return was won with dummy's ace and Meckstroth proceeded to cash his remaining winners in diamonds and spades. This end position was soon before him:

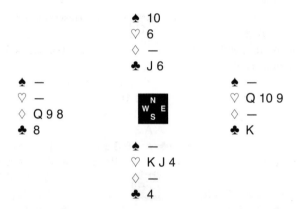

```
                    ♠ 10
                    ♡ 6
                    ♢ —
                    ♣ J 6
     ♠ —                          ♠ —
     ♡ —                          ♡ Q 10 9
     ♢ Q 9 8        N             ♢ —
     ♣ 8          W   E           ♣ K
                    S
                    ♠ —
                    ♡ K J 4
                    ♢ —
                    ♣ 4
```

Dummy's last trump left Blum with no good discard. He threw a heart, hoping for the best, but Meckstroth discarded his club loser and finessed the jack of hearts. The king and four of hearts provided two further tricks and the slam was his.

Blum gave a rueful nod of the head, acknowledging the fine dummy play. 'If you run the opening lead to your hand you go down,' he observed.

Meckstroth smiled as he reached for his pack of Marlboros. 'If anyone in this field makes that mistake, I'll give up smoking,' he said.

Rodwell, a passionate anti-smoker, affected a look of great surprise. 'You mean it?' he asked.

'Of course not,' Meckstroth replied.

Although there was little they could have done about it, Blum and Shafer ended up losing the match 33-17. With just one match to go, they had dropped to fifth place. Not bad, thought Blum. Indeed it was very good in a field packed with world champions. The prize money went down to eighth place but it would just be so great if they could finish in the top three.

The last match of the Macallan Pairs saw Blum and Schafer facing the legendary Brazilians, Gabriel Chagas and Marcelo Branco. This had not been one of their better tournaments and they were lying only halfway. On the first board Chagas arrived in a slam.

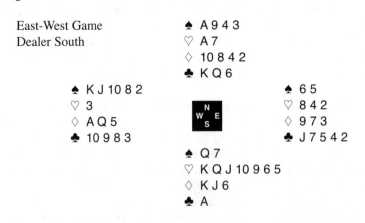

East-West Game	♠ A 9 4 3
Dealer South	♡ A 7
	◇ 10 8 4 2
	♣ K Q 6

♠ K J 10 8 2		♠ 6 5
♡ 3		♡ 8 4 2
◇ A Q 5		◇ 9 7 3
♣ 10 9 8 3		♣ J 7 5 4 2

	♠ Q 7
	♡ K Q J 10 9 6 5
	◇ K J 6
	♣ A

West	North	East	South
Schafer	**Branco**	**Blum**	**Chagas**
-	-	-	1♡
1♠	Dble	Pass	4♡
Pass	6♡	All Pass	

Schafer led ♣10 and Chagas won with the bare ace. He surveyed the dummy with his piercing brown eyes, calculating how to play the slam. There were eleven tricks on top and if East held the diamond queen a finesse of the jack of diamonds would yield a twelfth trick. The Brazilian was not inclined to play in this way. Only eleven points were out and West had made a vulnerable overcall. If anything, he was a favourite to hold the diamond queen. A better idea was to play for a strip squeeze, hoping to read which cards West had kept.

Chagas crossed to dummy with the ace of trumps and took the slight risk of cashing the two more club winners. Both defenders followed suit and he threw the six and jack of diamonds. Five further rounds of trumps brought him to this end position:

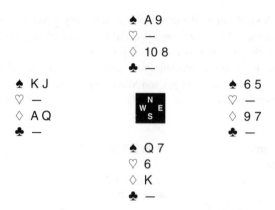

                        ♠ A 9
                        ♡ —
                        ◊ 10 8
                        ♣ —

    ♠ K J   ♠ 6 5
    ♡ —   N   ♡ —
    ◊ A Q   W   E   ◊ 9 7
    ♣ —   S   ♣ —

                        ♠ Q 7
                        ♡ 6
                        ◊ K
                        ♣ —

Chagas now led his last trump. Since Schafer had started with the three intermediate cards (♠J, ♣10, ◊Q), there had been no possibility of disguising which cards he had retained. Had he thrown the diamond queen at any stage, declarer would simply have knocked out the ace of diamonds to set up dummy's ◊10. Similarly, if had thrown the jack and 10 of spades, baring the king, declarer would have led the spade queen to set up a second spade trick.

As it was, Shafer had no good discard on the last trump. If he bared the diamond ace, he would be thrown in with a diamond to lead away from the king of spades. Taking his only chance – that East held the spade queen rather than South – he discarded the jack of spades on declarer's last trump. 'Diamond away,' said Chagas.

The ace of spades dropped West's king and the spade queen brought the Brazilian's total to twelve tricks. He conceded the last trick to the diamond ace but the slam was his.

Schafer looked unhappily across the table. 'I knew it was hopeless,' he said.

'Yes, yes, everyone will make it,' said Chagas, smiling broadly. 'One or two may not bid it, of course.'

The cards continued to run high. Unfortunately for the American pair, it was the opponents who held the big hands and were therefore in control. The sixth board in the set was another possible slam.

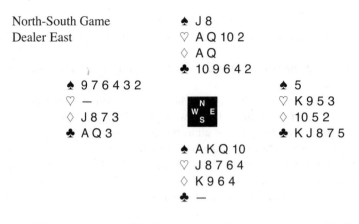

North-South Game	♠ J 8
Dealer East	♡ A Q 10 2
	◇ A Q
	♣ 10 9 6 4 2

♠ 9 7 6 4 3 2		♠ 5
♡ —		♡ K 9 5 3
◇ J 8 7 3		◇ 10 5 2
♣ A Q 3		♣ K J 8 7 5

	♠ A K Q 10
	♡ J 8 7 6 4
	◇ K 9 6 4
	♣ —

West	North	East	South
Schafer	**Branco**	**Blum**	**Chagas**
-	-	Pass	1♡
2♠	3NT	Pass	4♣
Pass	4◇	Pass	4♠
Pass	6♡	All Pass	

Branco's 3NT response showed a sound raise to game in hearts with no side-suit singleton. Three cue bids later the Brazilians were in a small slam.

Chagas won with the spade lead with the ace and played a trump. When West showed out he sat back in his chair to consider the implications of this. To rise with dummy's ace now would cost the contract. He knew from the bidding that East would ruff if he tried to reach his hand with a second round of spades. Suppose he cashed dummy's top diamonds and played for a diamond ruff in dummy. He would have to use a club ruff as the entry for this. He would then lose control when he drove out the king of trumps and was forced with another club.

Marcelo Branco waited patiently to hear what card he should play from the dummy to the second trick. 'Play the trump queen,' said Chagas eventually.

Blum allowed the queen to win and Chagas continued with dummy's two of trumps. If East ducked again, declarer would simply draw a third round of trumps with the ace and play on the side suits, eventually ruffing his last diamond in dummy. After some thought Blum rose with the trump king and switched to a club.

Chagas was not troubled by this. Indeed, he had already decided to play the contract on reverse dummy lines. He ruffed the club switch in his hand and crossed to a diamond honour to take a second club ruff. He then overtook his jack of trumps with dummy's ace and drew Blum's last trump with the ten. Chagas discarded his diamond loser on this trick and faced his remaining cards, which were now high.

Blum sighed as he wrote down the score. 'Nothing I could do, was there?' he asked.

The Brazilian turned his shining eyes in Blum's direction. 'No need for you to worry at all,' he informed him. 'I ruff two clubs whatever you do.'

The last match was not going at all to Blum's intended plan. The big hands were falling to North-South and they had a world-class declarer at the helm. What chance did that give to the unfortunate occupants of the East-West seats?

The pattern was not to be broken and the final board of the event saw Chagas declaring his third slam of the match. This was the deal:

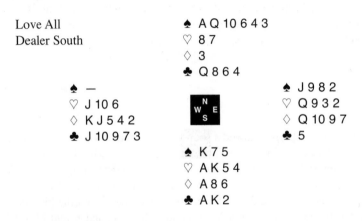

Love All
Dealer South

North
♠ A Q 10 6 4 3
♥ 8 7
◊ 3
♣ Q 8 6 4

West
♠ —
♥ J 10 6
◊ K J 5 4 2
♣ J 10 9 7 3

East
♠ J 9 8 2
♥ Q 9 3 2
◊ Q 10 9 7
♣ 5

South
♠ K 7 5
♥ A K 5 4
◊ A 8 6
♣ A K 2

West	North	East	South
Schafer	**Branco**	**Blum**	**Chagas**
-	-	-	2NT
Pass	3♥	Pass	3♠
Pass	5♠	Pass	6♠
All Pass			

Branco opted for the simple slam try of 5♠ and Chagas had an easy raise to the slam with his array of top cards. The jack of clubs was led and Chagas won with the ace. If trumps were 2-2 there would be thirteen easy tricks, since dummy's last club could be ruffed. If trumps were 3-1, or 4-0 onside, there would be twelve easy tricks. The Brazilian therefore gave his full attention to what could be done when the trumps were 4-0 offside. It seemed that in this case he might need the king of trumps to overruff East on the fourth round of clubs.

His mind made up, Chagas led a low trump to dummy's ace. West did indeed show out and the Brazilian declarer continued with a diamond to the ace and a diamond ruff. A heart to the ace was followed by a second diamond ruff.

'Small club,' said Chagas.

Blum summoned his concentration for one last time. What would happen if he ruffed in, expending his natural trump trick on a losing club? It seemed that declarer would have a counter to any return. On a diamond return, for example, he would ruff in his hand and throw a club from dummy. After cashing the bare king of trumps, he could reach dummy with a heart ruff to draw the outstanding trump.

Blum decided to throw a heart instead of ruffing. Chagas scored the king of clubs and led a third round of the suit, covering West's ten with dummy's queen. Blum ruffed and surveyed this end position:

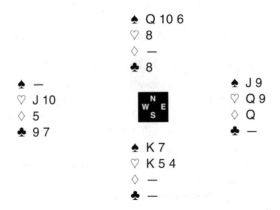

After a full three minutes of thought Blum had come to no firm conclusion. If he had read the cards correctly, it seemed that declarer was bound to make the contract. Eventually he exited with the nine of trumps.

Chagas won with the ten in dummy and crossed to the king of hearts to ruff a heart with the six. 'I make the last two trumps separately,' he announced.

With a sinking feeling Blum returned his cards to the wallet. It had seemed easy, the way Chagas had played it, but the timing had been quite delicate. There would surely be several pairs who had either failed to bid the slam or had gone down.

Somewhat apprehensively, Blum and Shafer walked towards the VuGraph room, where the commentators would have the latest news of all the scores. Was it possible that the other North-South pairs had performed as strongly as the Brazilians? If so, there was a tiny chance that they could hold on to a position in the top five.

The VuGraph room was packed and the two Americans had to stand at the back.

'We have most of the results from the last round now,' announced Barry Rigal. 'The most surprising is a 45-5 hammering of Blum and Shafer by Chagas and Branco. The Brazilians will move up several places. It looks as if Blum and Shafer will fall to about eighth place.'

Knowing that the nearby spectators were looking at him, Blum steeled himself to show no reaction to this news. A 45-5 loss? Jeez! So far as he could see, there wasn't a single thing they could have done about it. The Chagas guy had played the spots off the cards – just at the wrong moment.

Shafer grabbed Blum's arm and they walked out together into an empty corridor. 'We'd have settled for eighth place when we arrived here, Jerry,' he said.

'Yes, yes, I know,' Blum replied. 'But... we were lying third not so long ago.'

'We've had a great time, don't forget that,' continued Shafer, looking Blum in the eyes. 'Don't tell me it wasn't more fun than playing with Rick Winter or that terrible guy in Florida. What's his name? Dan something.'

'Dan Lerner, you mean?' Blum replied. 'He's not so bad. I come better than half-way when I play with him, I can tell you!'

Shafer laughed. 'Yeah, I guess he wasn't available,' he said. 'Come on, let's go the hospitality room. It's only good manners to support the sponsor. Let's drown our sorrows in that Macallan 10-year-old whisky.'

'I'm going to ask for it on the rocks with dry ginger,' said Blum. 'Do you think anyone will mind?'

Shafer laughed again. 'Probably not,' he replied. 'I'll let you ask first, though!'